ENDORSEMENTS

I0530421

You Can't Be Like Jonah is a heart-stirring and transformative exploration of faith, purpose, and divine calling. With poignant storytelling and practical wisdom, Harris invites readers to confront their own "Jonah moments," when fear, doubt, or resistance keep us from walking in obedience to God's plan. This is a beautifully written and deeply inspiring book that will leave readers feeling empowered, encouraged, and ready to say "yes" to God's call. Jennifer Jaye has given the world a gem that reminds us all of the power of obedience and the boundless reach of God's love.

Terrie Harris, Speaker and
Author of *Resilience in the Face of Loss*

Have you ever read a book that truly made an impact on your life? *You Can't Be Like Jonah, Twelve Hundred Miles to Obedience*, will bless you immeasurably and leave you wanting for more! Prepare for your mind to be renewed, your heart to be restored, and your spirit to be refreshed as you read Jennifer's incredible story.

Rev. Dr. Terry E. Mackey, Jr.
Pastor, Pilgrim Rest Baptist Church, Phoenix

You Can't Be Like Jonah is a heartfelt and faith-filled journey of obedience, healing, and unwavering trust in God. Jennifer Jaye's story inspires me to lean into faith when life feels impossible and to listen for God's direction even when it's unexpected or uncomfortable. This book isn't just a testimony—it's a guide for recognizing God's voice, resisting the enemy's lies, and boldly stepping into the calling He's placed on your life. I'm personally grateful to Jennifer Jaye for her transparency and wisdom, which have challenged me to grow in my walk with God. Whether you're seeking encouragement or a deeper connection with Him, this book will bless you in ways you didn't know you needed."

Rev. Dr. Seth Martin
Director of Formation, Sanctuary
Minneapolis

JENNIFER JAYE

YOU CAN'T BE LIKE

JONAH

TWELVE HUNDRED MILES TO OBEDIENCE

Study Guide Included for Personal or Group Discussion

You Can't Be Like Jonah
Twelve Hundred Miles to Obedience
Jennifer Jaye

To contact the author:
Jenniferjaye67@gmail.com
youtube.com/movingforward1265

Published by:

Mary Ethel

Mary Ethel Eckard
Frisco, Texas

Library of Congress Control Number: 2024923449
ISBN (Print): 979-8-9910210-5-0
ISBN (E-book): 979-8-9910210-6-7

Cover photo taken by Nicole Selleck

DEDICATION

To my mother, lovingly known as Grandma Sue.
She came up with my pen name many years ago.

My mom taught me much about life:
the importance of education, fortitude, faith, and grit.
Without those lessons, this would be a very different story.

Mom, this one is in memory of you.

ACKNOWLEDGEMENTS

I am indebted to Pastor Venshard Dobbins. Though he didn't yet know me, his prophetic words confirmed that I am to share my story. His words, "God told me to tell you to write the book," rang in my heart throughout the process, reminding me this was of God and not of myself.

Thank you to my Circle of 12, a group of twelve women who came together (virtually) to commit to pray for my God-called journey every day. Their friendship, encouragement, and constant support and prayers have carried me through this process.

Thank you to Nicole Selleck, the first friend I made in Phoenix. She became my accountability coach the first year of writing and has been invaluable to me as an encouragement and friend.

Special thanks to my editor, Mary Ethel Eckard, for her insightful guidance, friendship, and encouragement throughout this process.

My sincere appreciation to my sisters for their constant love and understanding.

All my love to my children and grandchildren who inspired me with their love and support, even though I moved so very far away.

Finally, to my husband Howard who has been a constant source of encouragement and accountability. Without his endless patience, I may not have completed writing and publishing this book in this timeline.

CONTENTS

PREFACE

A Thousand Ways to Die in Arizona

Around the time Covid19 hit the world, I stepped into a new place of discovering who I am and who God created me to be. He did this by opening my spiritual eyes and ears to seeing and hearing who He is and how my life is to be centered in obedience to Him. In essence, He wanted me to move from Kansas to Arizona, 1200 miles away from everyone and everything I knew, so that He could use me in new ways.

As you read this book, you will understand many things about my life, from childhood to present day. It's written from a 20/20 hindsight perspective as I look back as an adult to the way my upbringing shaped me. No regrets, no shame. God used everything to bring me full circle to where I am today.

When I first got to Arizona, I quickly learned there were things to be careful of. Like, things that could actually kill you. Scorpions, spiders, snakes… the usual things you might think of. I jokingly said I was going to write a book called *A Thousand Ways To Die In Arizona*. I started making a list.

Way #127: Bears. Apparently, there are bears in the area. I saw a news article shortly after moving that one had been spotted in the zip code I lived in! Stay indoors. Noted.

Way #256: Javelina. Who knew these things lived in the outskirts of Phoenix? These vicious, wild boar-like animals have sharp tusks and are very strong. When I first arrived, there was one report each week for four weeks of attacks on humans. These rabies carriers are no joke.

Way #332: Jaguars. Yep. Jaguars. I know, right? But there is one they have been tracking for seven years still roaming the mountains of Phoenix. They named him El Jefe. Note to self: never hike after sunset!

Way #401: Toads. You read that right. Toads. There are toxic toads in Arizona. The Sonoran Desert toad lives underground most of the year but comes out to mate in late August; they literally invade like a plague! They excrete a poisonous toxin that can cause a rash and severe illness, or even death, if ingested. I wouldn't go ingesting a frog, but I guess because it can cause a psychedelic experience, some people would. Gross.

Way #571: Heat. The temperature in the summer can get in the 120's. That means the temperature in a car is near 170 degrees! Shaded parking spots can be difficult to find. Do not leave people in the car without the a/c running!

Way #624: Pencil Cacti. The sap from this particular cactus is poisonous if you're allergic to latex, and of course I am. It may cause seizures, coma, and even death!

Way #740: Dehydration/Heat Exhaustion. The heat is extreme in the summertime, and I learned quickly to always have extra water in my car. The traffic can be terrible, so don't be caught without enough water. Hats are also necessary. Too bad if you like your cute hairdo. Wear a hat. Skin cancer is also a thing!

Way #819: Car Wrecks. These can happen anywhere, but there seem to be more in Arizona than in Kansas. The wrecks seem to be major and shut down highways for hours. I did some searching on Google and discovered Arizona is sixth on the list of states with the most car wrecks. People on bicycles or walking are especially at risk.

Way #958: Falling off a mountain (hike with care). People fall into the Grand Canyon every year. Then there are people who simply fall while hiking because tennis shoes are not proper for hiking in Arizona. Wear proper footwear.

Way #1,000: Valley Fever. Apparently, there is a fungus that lives in the soil in the southwestern United States. When inhaled it can cause deadly infections. People aged 60 and older are most susceptible. Indeed, I am 60.

As I began writing my story, I saw how these thousand ways have, in some sense, been chasing me my entire life, though in different places and in different ways. Using hindsight vision, I've woven them into my story hoping the reader will see and understand some of the ways Satan tries to rob us of the abundant blessings of living for God alone.

But don't get me wrong. I am not writing this to tell you how to survive in Arizona. More accurately, I am writing this in hopes that you will discover how to hear God's voice, how to recognize the lies of the devil, and to inspire you to survive this world by following God through obedience in all things without fear.

A bit of my history is necessary so that you grasp where I was in my head and my heart when Jesus called me to move.

INTRODUCTION

God has rescued me from many challenges too big to navigate without His help. For many years the enemy tried to silence me and keep me from my destiny. This book is a compilation of my life journey, sharing how God convinced me to move an unfathomable twelve hundred miles from everything and everyone I knew and loved. But He did not just spring this unexpected relocation on me out of the blue. He had a purpose and plan for my life even before I was conceived. That plan started unfolding, bit by bit, on the day I was born even though I was unaware of it.

God was doing a new thing in me right then, just like He is doing a new thing in you right now. I hope you are listening, praying, and reading the Word. You cannot know His voice if you are not listening. You, likewise, won't recognize His voice unless you are spending time with Him regularly and often.

My pastor and friend, Rick, said, "Change is coming. He's doing new things. Find your purpose." I knew I had found my purpose but obeying God meant moving away from the family I loved dearly. Pastor Rick also said, "Don't believe the lies!" He was referring to Satan, the father of lies,[1] who has been twisting God's Word from the beginning.

I've come too far. I can't look back. "Did God *really* tell you to leave everything you know and love?" Yes! Yes, He did! Emphatically, Yes. I stepped out in obedience with my focus on Him, and off I went.

I am sharing my journey and how His plan rolled out through things the world might call a coincidence. Perhaps my story will help you discover how to hear God's voice, how to recognize the lies of Satan, and inspire you to follow God through obedience in all things without fear. Because, spoiler alert, He has a purpose for your life, too!

> *"Then, the Word of the Lord came to me saying,*
> *'Before I formed you in the womb I knew you,*
> *before you were born, I sanctified you;*
> *I ordained you a prophet to the nations.'*
> *Then said I, 'Ah Lord God, behold I cannot speak for I am a youth,*
> *but the Lord said to me, 'Do not say, "I am a youth"*
> *for you shall go to all whom I send you and*
> *whatever I command you, you shall speak.*
> *Do not be afraid of their faces for I am with you,*
> *to deliver you,' says the Lord.*
> *Then the Lord put forth His hand to touch my mouth*
> *and the Lord said to me, 'Behold, I have put My words in your mouth.'"*
> Jeremiah 1:4-9 NKJV

To grasp why I said yes when Jesus called me to move, turn the page and step into my story.

CHAPTER

1

Faith Building in Childhood

When Mama was three years old, her father died suddenly of a perforated ulcer. Though I'm fuzzy on what happened to her mom, I know she was an alcoholic. Mama and her siblings were taken away by the state of Missouri in the late 1940s. My mama and her only sister were placed together in a Catholic orphanage for girls. The beginning of my mama's life was difficult, to say the least. Though I won't share the details, I will give a general overview.

When Mama was eight years old, she was adopted and isolated from her biological siblings. When she was fourteen, she was forced into a marriage with my father. Over the next nine years, she gave birth to six children; five girls and a boy. I am number five in birth order with four older sisters and one younger brother.

Mama, abused by my father, spent her life pretending to be someone she wasn't. She was afraid to talk to anyone about the abuse because she didn't want the state to take us away, having experienced firsthand the orphanage system. At the same time, she must have been as afraid of Dad as I was.

The foundational years of my childhood with my father were built on dysfunction and abuse. Thankfully, he was away a lot. At the age of five, I didn't want him to come home and I worried every day that he would.

This birthed within my heart a fear of what lay ahead; a terror of the future. When he didn't come home, I worried I would wake up in the night to find him in my bed. I was afraid of the future because, eventually, he did come home; eventually, he did come to my bed. He sexually molested me on a regular basis for fourteen years, sometimes in front of my brother.[3] I was beginning to understand the ugliness that was my father.

By the time I was ten, my mother moved us across town to a tiny rental house with filthy threadbare carpet and too few bedrooms for everyone. While we kids doubled up two to a room, Mama took the sofa. She also took a job and, for the first time I can remember, we lived without my father. Still, he would show up occasionally and throw his weight around staying a day, a week, or two weeks. Those were awful times. The rest of the time was better though fear of his return always loomed. Finally, my mother put a stop to his unannounced visits. She stood toe to toe with him and told him not to ever come back. And for three years, he didn't.

When we moved to that little rental house, Mama did not waste time feeling sorry for herself or her situation. She picked herself up, made a plan, and got a job at a discount store where she worked during the day. In the evenings she attended school to earn her high school diploma, which she received at the age of 33.

Mama moved up the ranks at that discount center, all the way to assistant store manager! Eventually she opened her own store in downtown Lawrence, Kansas, and became successful in the business world. She did her best to raise her six kids to know and love the Lord in spite of the trauma, fear, and insecurity she was fighting.

We didn't have two nickels to rub together, and everything was complicated. Sometimes we didn't have food, and other times we would eat the same thing every night. One day we came home to find a 50-pound bag of potatoes on the porch, so we ate potato soup until they were gone. And we were grateful.

Also, Mama washed our clothes in the bathtub and wrung them by hand because we only had enough money for the clothes dryer at the laundromat. When our landlord finally provided a used washing machine, it broke down frequently. I recall one evening Mama was near tears (or a mental breakdown). I stood in the dimly lit hallway with my younger brother staring wide-eyed at her. We had never seen her like this. She was always a "glass half full" kind of person. But on this night, she had her hands on the washer, her head hung low between her shoulders, and she let out a noise filled with anguish. The washing machine was broken again. Mama had six kids, homework, and she had worked all day. She didn't have the time or energy to kneel on the hard bathroom floor to a tub filled with dirty laundry. She began to pray. Afterward, she turned the knob on the washing machine, and it began filling with water!

We were learning the power of prayer.

Somehow Mama managed to get a car. The 1966 Ford Mustang was mostly rust colored with the exception of one bright blue fender. It also had a hole in the front passenger floorboard so whoever sat in the front seat had to put their foot over it to prevent water or rocks from flying into the car. There were seven in our family with a car that seated four, so Mama took us to school in shifts. A few days after the washing machine incident, that little sports car wouldn't start. It was cold outside, and Mom was irritated again. My brother and I shouted, "Lay your hands on it and pray, Mama!" She looked up from under the uplifted hood of the car where she was surveying the engine and gave a sigh.[4] We reminded her how prayer worked with the washing machine. We kept at her until finally she looked at us with resignation and dropped the hood of the car allowing it to slam shut. She laid her hands on it and prayed silently. Then she opened her car door without saying a word and slid back into the driver's seat as we all held our breath in hope. When she turned the ignition, the car engine sputtered and came to life. We cheered for God and said, "We told you! You just had to pray!"

My siblings and I were raised in the Catholic faith, and we attended parochial school from first through sixth grades. We prayed rote prayers but through these situations, God was building my faith and showing me how I can count on Him if only I will come to Him with my prayers.

A New Home, A New Life

During the three years my father was away, on August 21, 1974, The Equal Credit Opportunity Act was passed. That meant women could get credit or a loan without a man. It's hard to fathom this happened in my lifetime, but true to her nature, Mama grabbed the brass ring! She was a pioneer and a go-getter! Sometimes I wonder how she found the energy to keep going from all the crazy hours she worked and the extreme pressure to live as a single woman in those times. She persevered by refreshing herself with good friends and handling the heat with a good work ethic. She was approved for a zero down home loan and closed on our newly built house within the year! Mama taught me how to go after what I wanted, and I wanted to be a cheerleader like she had been. If she could buy a house with no down payment and no man required, then I could chase my dream of being a cheerleader.

The new house was in a neighboring town which meant I had to change schools and the girls at the new school were mean. They called me awful names even though they didn't know me. They only knew what they saw. I was so much more, but how could they know that?

That same year, I had my first taste of victory. Mama had been a cheerleader, and she wanted at least one of her girls to have that same experience. I think it was one of the few fond memories she had as a child. When I was in the 8th grade, girls trying out for cheerleaders had to perform individually on the school stage in front of the cheerleaders from the University of Kansas.[5] The backstage area was in the shadows and dimly lit. It smelled musty from the heavy red velvet curtains that hung in the auditorium for decades. As I waited for my turn, filled with nervous excitement, someone handed me a small piece of white paper neatly folded in half. I quickly opened it to find it simply said, "Good luck. Mom." I was extremely happy she took the time to call the school and leave me those sweet words of encouragement.

As I refolded the note, my number was called. I shoved Mama's encouragement inside my right tube sock, then ran onto the large, empty stage, smiling through the anxiety. Performing the required cheer, I mistakenly ended it with my hands lifted straight up instead of holding them in the required high V. I stood in shock, holding the lift like it was intentional, hoping no one noticed. Then as I bounded off the stage, I cheered and pumped my fists, still grinning as if nothing had gone wrong.

After the last contestant tried out, we were led by the cheer squad into a classroom to await the final cut. I found a desk at the back of the room and anxiously waited. Most of the girls were chatting excitedly, but I was silent, wanting to know the outcome, trying to harness my insecurities. I was from a poor family. I had friends but I wasn't popular. I was not the stereotypical rich and pretty cheerleader people imagined.

As name after name was called, I was sure I hadn't made the team, so I put my head on my folded arms resting on the desk. Just as my head connected with my forearms, my name was called. I made the team!

That evening when I got home, I went to my bedroom and thanked Jesus. I was so incredibly happy. I made the cheerleader team for my ninth-grade year, fulfilling the dream of both me and my mom. I remember telling Jesus that if He were there in person, I would hug Him because I finally knew what it felt like to love someone. I loved Him. At thirteen, I had been afraid of people all my life. Finally, because of Jesus, I understood what it was to love.

A Thousand Ways to Die in Arizona
Way #127: Bears

I saw a news article shortly after moving to Arizona. A bear had been spotted in the zip code where I live. There are black bears in Arizona, but they can also be the color of brown, tan, or cinnamon. Black bears are associated with primal instincts and aggression. These bears may stalk someone when hiking or they may attack and/or kill to protect their cubs. In the heat of summer, they go in search of water. Hence why they were in backyard pools.

Don't sleep outside on the patio sofa, especially if you have a pool, even if the stars are amazing and the weather is perfect. Also, stay indoors and do not sleep with the windows open. Alexa, lock the doors.

Long before moving to Arizona, I realized my mama was a Mama Bear. She would go to battle for her children, she would search out everything we needed, and she would come against anything or anyone wanting to cause us harm. I also learned she is a strong, resilient, brave woman who would push ahead, through all kinds of adversity, to find her way and make sure her children grew up with Jesus in our hearts. From her early childhood until the time she found her voice and courage, she was trampled over. But when she found her voice, she rose up and got us out of the situation we were in. Like a bear on the prowl, she would not be denied.

She is my favorite Mama Bear. She saved my life by the decisions she made. Through her, I learned to love the Lord. Through my own life choices, I also learned the consequences that come when we don't walk in obedience to God. But somehow, by the grace of God, at some point in my early life, I was gifted with a heart that was bent toward obedience. It would just take a while to discover that truth.

REFLECTION

1. Read Jeremiah 1:4-9, putting your name in the verse in place of the word "you." What new insights do you gain about yourself and God's plan for you from these verses?

2. The enemy tried to stamp out my mama's voice from an early age by sending her into an orphanage and then into the arms of an abusive man. But she was able to break free and find her significance in life through faith. How about you? Do you trust God to help you rise above the situations, circumstances, and people who try to keep you down?

3. I learned resilience, courage, and the power of prayer by watching my mama. Are you modeling godly characteristics someone can imitate to bring them closer to God?

4. Even in my childhood, the enemy tried to silence me and cause me to doubt there was a plan and purpose for my life. If you doubt God's love for you and His purpose and destiny for your life, journal a prayer below, asking Him to reveal to you the truth of who you are.

5. Satan is known as the father of lies. He twists and turns everything good and speaks negative words into our minds. His plan is to destroy you and keep you feeling small and insignificant. What lies does he speak to you that you can cast down today by replacing them with the truth of God's Word?

6. Read 2 Samuel 17:8. Can you picture that mama bear? The wild eyes, the loud, throaty groan, the head swiveling from side to side in search? Have you ever had a time in your life when you felt desperate like the bear mentioned in this verse? How did you handle it? If you could do it over again, would you handle the situation differently?

CHAPTER

2

Knowing and Experiencing God

As I was growing up, I felt Jesus nearby. I heard His promptings and recognized His voice. Even in my wilder teenage years, I wanted Him and desired to be close to Him. I didn't know how to make that happen, and I didn't have friends to turn to who could help me learn more. Some of the kids in high school attended Youth for Christ gatherings each week. They invited a few students to go with them, but as much as I wanted to go, I was not invited, and I was too shy to invite myself.

I attended high school with Eric R., the football star who was cute, popular, played guitar, and was a partier. One day Eric was invited to a Youth for Christ event where he was saved. All the kids at school talked about him saying things like, "Boy, is he going to be sorry when he wakes up and realizes what he has done!" Eric never regretted it.

He and I didn't talk much because he ran with a different crowd, but I watched him from a distance, marveling at the difference in him. I didn't know what being saved meant, but I did notice that Eric's life changed drastically. He got rid of his t-shirts with naughty words and slogans, he broke his inappropriate record albums, and he carried and read a Bible. He continued to walk with the Lord, and his new life decisions and the overnight change in him made an impact on me. [6]

I was happy for Eric. It was at this tender young age that I decided if I ever had children, I would name the child after him – Eric if a boy, Erica if a girl. I wanted my child to walk with the Lord and impact others just like Eric had impacted me.

Though I was watching Eric and seeing the change in his life, I wasn't understanding how he changed; just that he had. I wanted someone to make me feel safe and loved, even if just for a night, so I began drinking, smoking, and eventually sleeping around. Right out of high school, at 17 and immature, I enrolled at the University of Kansas. I attended one spring semester, and I never used drugs, but with zero accountability I majored in skipping class and day drinking. It was not the best time in my life. I dropped out after one semester and life hit me. At nineteen, I became pregnant outside of marriage. My baby's father left town when he found out, saying he wanted no future with us. We never saw him again.

One Sunday, seeking to draw nearer to Jesus, I walked ten blocks to attend a Catholic church. Everyone knew me. They knew I was unwed, and they ignored me. In fact, one woman pursed her pinkly painted lips, glanced sideways at me, then clutched her white patent leather purse to her chest and turned away, seemingly in disgust. Well before the service began, embarrassed and self-conscious, I pushed open the heavy glass door and walked out of the church. Tears stung my eyes as I determined not to cry until I returned home. Needless to say, I never went back.

My pregnancy due date was July 12, 1982. I was barely 20 years old. Still single, clueless and without a car, I spent the night with my friend, Cheryl, who was worried about me. On July 11, I woke up early with contractions. Beginning at 6 a.m., I placed a call to the hospital every two hours, each time being told to call back in two hours with an update. At noon, I asked Cheryl to take me to the hospital only to be greeted by an irritated nurse who wanted to know why I was there when she told me to wait.

The nurses decided to check my progress before sending me home. I had dilated to 2 cm. They said if I could walk the halls and dilate to 4 cm, I could stay. Walking up and down hospital halls was boring. I had to stop every few minutes and hold onto the wall until the contraction passed. I did a lot of thinking and praying during that hour. I knew about God, and I knew about prayer. I didn't know Jesus as my own personal Savior and I certainly wasn't living for Him, but boy was I talking to Him.

Up and down the cold, white tile floors of Lawrence Memorial Hospital, I prayed something I had prayed a thousand times during the last nine months. "Lord, please help my child be blessed like Eric. Help my child to love You with all their being. Help my child to live unashamed of You. Help my child to follow Eric's example and serve You." At 11:10 p.m., my baby boy, Eric Lee, came into this world.[7]

By the age of twenty-two, I decided to marry a man without knowing he had so many issues of his own. I knew he drank alcohol when we married, but I didn't realize it was a problem until after we were married. When I discovered he was a heroin addict, I was mortified. Every time he told me it was the last time, I believed him. The arguments, betrayal, and fear of him coming home "in a mood" fed my fear of the future that developed during childhood and still hung over me like a black cloud.

Married and pregnant with my second child, I started attending a small non-denominational church in the downtrodden strip mall a couple blocks from our duplex. We had one car that my husband needed for work, so I put my son in his red Radio Flyer wagon and pulled him the two blocks to church. It was there in that makeshift sanctuary with white tile floors and metal folding chairs that I first heard the gospel message.

I knew the Bible stories from elementary school, but this was different. This gospel said I could be a friend of Jesus, and I could have the Holy Spirit living in me. This was the best news ever! I wasn't sure what the pastor was asking of me when he gave the invitation, so I didn't walk forward. But on that day, I heartily accepted Jesus Christ as my personal Savior.[8]

My son, Lance, was born soon after and we attended this church regularly. I wanted my children saturated in God's love, and I wanted them surrounded by Christians who could help me raise them in His Word.

A Thousand Ways to Die in Arizona
Way #256: Javelina

When I first arrived in Arizona, I was told to be careful of the javelina. These pig looking mammals with extremely sharp tusks have poor eyesight but a great sense of smell, and they are very strong. They can carry rabies, distemper, or salmonella. I did not know what a javelina was, but I was going to google that and find out!

Barely in Arizona for a month, the local news headline was, "Javelina jumps into car. Welcome to Arizona!" I was not humored as they warned viewers to keep car doors shut and locked. There was one report each week for four weeks of attacks on humans. While it is true you won't likely die from a javelina bite, you will die from bleeding out from the bite. Who cares about that distinction? Dead is dead, after all.

"Dead is dead, after all" is not true for accepting Christ and being baptized. There is a distinct difference between being baptized as an infant (someone else making the decision for the baby) and being baptized once one is old enough to make the decision for themselves (accepting Jesus as their Lord and Savior). Scripture clearly says in John 3:3 *"In reply Jesus declared, 'I tell you the truth, no one can see the kingdom of God unless he is born again."* And in John 3:15, *"everyone who believes in Him will have eternal life."* This openly states the person must believe and receive Jesus. An infant doesn't have the understanding yet to make this decision. However, once a child is old enough to believe for themselves, then salvation and baptism are an act of obedience to Christ. *"Therefore, go and make disciples of all nations, baptizing them in the name of the Father and of the Son and of the Holy Spirit"* Matthew 28:19. And then, even after we die a natural life, our spirit lives eternally with God!

Being a believer didn't mean my life was going smoothly. I was married to a husband who was an alcoholic and a heroin addict. He was barely twenty when we married, and I knew he liked to go to keg parties. I did not realize it was a problem until later. I also did not know he used drugs. I was so naïve and when he told me he had used drugs for the last time, I believed him. This was the proverbial bite. Our marriage was bleeding out and I didn't know it.

REFLECTION

1. I felt looked over and left out when classmates failed to invite me to Youth for Christ events. Is there anyone in your circle who needs an invitation to attend an event to hear the gospel of Jesus? Write their name below and commit to invite them to an upcoming event or church service with you.

2. Who in your life has influenced you by their walk with Christ? Journal a prayer of thanksgiving for them.

3. James 4:8 says when we come near to God, He will come near to us. Scripture teaches us that God is always pursuing us, but when we turn toward Him and begin to pursue Him, that's when we recognize His presence. Why do you think it takes our seeking Him to sense His presence?

4. At an early age, a fear of the future was deposited into my spirit and mind. That fear accompanied me for many years. The love of Christ was the victory over that fear. Do you have fears or traumas from your early years that need to be surrendered to Jesus for healing? Journal these below and ask Jesus to bring you victory through His abiding love and presence.

5. Have you given your heart to Jesus by believing in Him for salvation? Read Romans 3:23, Romans 5:8, Romans 6:23, Romans 8:1, and Romans 10:9 for a better understanding of how to receive salvation. Journal your questions. Then read the next chapter and find additional scripture that will give more information. If you still have questions, find a trusted Christian friend or a local pastor who can walk you through these scriptures.

6. Read Mark 5:11-16. Since pigs were unclean to the Jews, these had to be Gentiles tending the herd. Yet they went and told others about Jesus. Do you share what God has done in your life? If not, think of one person you could share with this week and write their name below.

CHAPTER

3

A New Ministry Unfolds

Being married to an addict is a difficult life. As a new believer, I thought it was my duty to honor my wedding vows to my husband and my God and stay married "until death do us part." I attended church every week. I volunteered to help with many events, prayer teams, and lock-ins for two reasons. The first was because I loved the Lord and wanted to do whatever I could to serve Him. The second was that I was miserable at home and didn't want to subject my two sons to their dad's drunken rants.

A few years later, eight months pregnant with my third child, I ventured to the pastor's office to ask some hard questions. How was I to love my husband through his addiction? How was I to stay encouraged in the Word? How was I to keep my vows? I was horrified when he counseled me to file for divorce. How could he suggest that? My mind was reeling as I left his office and walked into a Sunday School classroom. I sat on a cold, metal folding chair with tears stinging my eyes. The room was void of students, but the teacher sat at the white plastic folding table leaning forward on her elbows with concern in her eyes. To my 25-year-old self, this sixtyish woman seemed wise and trustworthy. With trembling lips, I explained to her what had transpired in the wood-paneled office across the hall. Her immediate indignation convinced me that I was right! I should not even consider divorce.

That week the pastor was fired. I later learned he was already on thin ice with the church board and this piece of information was the final straw. This woman I confided in shared my situation with the congregation. Why would she betray my trust? How could she? This was my first experience with church hurt and hurt it did.

Eric was six and Lance was four when Sarah was born. After Sarah was born, I would get the kids dressed on Sunday mornings and head to church. My husband didn't attend with us except on rare occasions. He didn't like church, or the things taught there, and he hid my Bible, forbidding me from reading it. But thanks be to God, I had one small leather bound Bible hidden in the laundry room cupboard that was my saving grace.

My husband worked a seasonal construction job, so he was home much of the winter. I would wait for him to pass out and then find my Bible and read and pray before he woke up. Drug addicts don't sleep much, so I had a three-hour window. Most nights, it was two or three in the morning when I could sneak out of the bedroom and read the words of my loving God. My nerves would be on edge as I tiptoed down the carpeted hall to retrieve my hidden treasure from behind the stack of neatly folded spare blankets above the matching washer and dryer. I would sit curled up at the corner of the secondhand sofa and read God's precious words as my anxious nerves settled down and peace flooded me. I am grateful that God kept me safe as I spent time with Him, night after night, year after year.

I daydreamed about what would happen if I left him. Where would I go and how would I survive? I imagined the kids and I would stay with my friend, Dixie. Then, the daydream became reality. After fifteen years of marriage and fifteen years of searching for a biblical reason to leave the emotionally and verbally abusive marriage, I finally understood that our safety was a priority. Eric was 16, Lance was 12, and Sarah was 9.

I pretended it was a normal morning. I fed the kids breakfast, got their backpacks ready, twisted Sarah's extremely long hair into her favorite braid, and kissed her goodbye as she hopped on the old yellow school bus. With the hills, we couldn't see the second bus headed to pick up the boys, but we recognized the trail of dust gathering in the air down the long gravel road. I told them they weren't getting on the bus that day. As they looked at me surprised, I explained that they needed to gather as much as they could, as quickly as they could, because we were leaving their dad.

They were both overjoyed! As they ran to get their things, I asked Lance to also get his sister's things. The two of them were close and played together a lot. I trusted him to know what to pack. As we got in the car, I prepared to go to my friend, Dixie's, but the Lord prompted me to go to the pastor's house. I wrestled with this in my mind as I traveled the 13 miles to town, but when the turn arrived on my left, I made it, trusting God entirely.

As we arrived, he and his wife were making their way out the door. Their hands were full of luggage and their eyes said they were checking off the mental list to ensure nothing was forgotten. They were leaving for a two week mission trip. When I told him I had left my husband, the pastor gave me the keys to his house, invited us to stay there, and encouraged me to be safe and not tell anyone where we were. Then they got in the car and drove away. And just like that, we had a safe place to stay, food to eat, and beds to sleep in without intruding on anyone. It gave me much-needed time to figure things out. (If you are living in an abusive situation there is help. Call 1-800-799-7233 or text BEGIN to 88788.)

Working through that season was scary. The boys had seen their father's ways, but Sarah had been protected from his anger because she was daddy's little girl, and she went to bed early, so she didn't experience his outbursts. This made our leaving hard for her to understand but, unfortunately, she saw his abuse during the weeks that followed.

After we left, my husband terrorized us. He threatened us, followed us, and tried to run me off the road, and said cruel, untrue, horrific things. After obtaining a restraining order and the right to move the kids back home, the police served him papers and forced him to leave the premises. After we moved back into the house, he continued to terrorize us by knocking on bedroom windows at night, shooting guns in the yard, killing our puppy, and other cruel things.

Two years after leaving, I married one of the police officers who came to our house on numerous calls. I wanted him to be a dream come true, my savior, so to speak. But he wasn't and, again, I felt trapped. My kids and I were unhappy because I ignored the red flags and chose to think he was the godly man I hoped for. Eric, then 18 years old, began drinking heavily and was angry that I married another man who couldn't show love toward him or his siblings. Our relationship was in a bad state of repair. It was during this time that he told me how his dad had held him at gunpoint when he was 10 years old. I grieved his broken heart and the fact that I was clueless about what had gone on inside my own home.

Stepping into the New

But God. He rescued Eric out of this lifestyle when he was 20. In 2002, Eric (20) and Sarah (14) went with our church youth group on a mission trip to Tempe, Arizona to go door-to-door and share the gospel.

Shortly after returning, our church youth leaders had a year-end planning meeting for the upcoming school term. Our youth group was small with about six students. Before the meeting, Sarah shared an idea with me that she wanted to present. I was one of the few parents who attended the meeting.

The cavernous classroom was filled with mismatched sofas and a few big pillows donated to the church. There was a mural painted on the wall that simply said JESUS and a whiteboard covered the opposite wall. Sarah was sitting on the couch next to me. When another girl, Angela, voiced the same idea Sarah had shared with me privately, it was remarkable. Sarah nodded in agreement with Angela and then she shared her thoughts.

While on their mission trip in Tempe, they had both heard a

phenomenal speaker from Texas named Thomas Young, and a fantastic band from Tennessee called Pierce. They wanted our church to host an event and invite all the other church youth groups to attend. Naturally, they wanted Thomas Young and Pierce to be the speaker and band.

In our small Kansas town, there was a large church with a sizable youth group and a greater budget. Events at that church were always large scale; they had giveaway prizes like mountain bikes and gaming stations. This large church was generous to invite our youth to all their events, however, this time, our youth wanted to do something they could invite them to attend.

The youth director, Martha, loved the idea but did not want to serve as the lead. She and her husband were already hosting youth group activities and felt they didn't have the bandwidth to add another event to their responsibilities. I volunteered thinking, how hard can it be to put an event together? I was about to find out.

Not being invited to the Youth for Christ events while I was in high school taught me to extend invitations to every young person and organization in the community. I wanted everyone to hear the gospel. We also wanted a free event so all youth could attend, and we wanted to feed them. Our budget didn't allow for the band and speaker the girls hoped for, but we were able to get some local bands and a great speaker, Eric R, from Youth for Christ. Remember him?

We advertised via word of mouth, posters, and newspaper ads. We collected donations through love offerings at church. We planned, and we prayed. I asked a woman, Racquel, to volunteer. She signed up to supply the cups and soon became my co-director and best friend for the ages!

Most importantly, the event was saturated in prayer. We prayed together daily, often at midnight after our families were taken care of. We had a weekly prayer meeting and invited all youth pastors in the county. Martha and Paul were my two faithful prayer warrior attendees each week. There were also others who joined us from time to time.

We called the event the Back 2 Skool Bash, or B2SB. When the date came for the event, the weather forecast called for rain. This was a concern because the stage and electronics were outdoors and we expected a lot of teens to attend, and they did. About 100 students showed up. We were ecstatic. This was a large group in comparison to our youth group of six. Students came out in the humidity and heat, and they stood around on our frequently patched but never resurfaced asphalt parking lot and visited with friends, played hacky sack, and waited for food.

My friend, Roger, grilled hotdogs and dumped them into a crock pot to keep them warm. Another friend, Richard, grabbed them from the crockpot with his small, silver tongs and placed them carefully into buns sitting open-faced on the flimsy paper plates in the hands of hungry teenagers. I was walking by to check on things when Richard leaned into me and said, while jutting his chin in the direction of the long line of yet unfed youth, "These are all the hotdogs we have left. There are no more. There are not enough." I encouraged him to keep filling plates, and I went off to pray. "*Ten hotdogs, fifty kids. Dear God.*"

When the event was over, Richard found me and said, "We never ran out of hotdogs. I didn't realize until the line was finished, and I remembered we didn't have enough. I just kept working and we never ran out! It was the miracle of the feeding of the hotdogs!" He was overjoyed and we laughed and praised God. We couldn't stop smiling.

Another miracle. It didn't rain. The storm moved backward. The weatherman explained to viewers that night on the ten o'clock news that winds move west to east in America. This storm system was, in fact, moving west to east until it reached the Miami County line, where we were praying for Him to hold off the rain. The weatherman excitedly showed his weather maps and explained that, in a rare phenomenon, the storm began to move backward. It moved backward for three hours (the length of our event).

Never, ever, doubt God.

Having invited Eric R. to speak at our inaugural event, I had the opportunity to tell him how his life choices after receiving Christ at 18 had impacted my life. I told him how I had pledged to name my firstborn after him, in hopes my child would follow Jesus as he had. Then I introduced my son, Eric, to his namesake. Eric R. was 41 years old when he heard how his 18-year-old choices changed my life. We never know who is watching us. We can be an example that others want to follow.

It was an amazing night. In addition to our personal connections with each other, we also saw three youth come to know Jesus. Their lives were forever changed because of our faithfulness to trust God.

We held B2SB in our patchwork parking lot again the next year with about the same results. The speaker was Andy Addis.[10] Then Raquel and I began to pray about a bigger space. We needed a larger venue.

In 2006 we moved the event to a middle school building auditorium that would hold **627** people. The fire marshal told us we could not have people in the orchestra pit or the aisles and everyone had to have a seat. So, we stationed two adults by the doors to take tickets and two more to count heads as students came in.

> "We didn't pray big enough. If we had an even larger venue, God would have filled it up."

The event was to begin at 6:30 p.m. At 6:15, hoping for 200 kids to attend, there was no one in line to enter. I panicked. What if nobody showed up? Just before the doors opened, kids started arriving and consuming food. As more and more kids entered the foyer through the heavy glass entrance, we wondered if we would get them all in. Well, God showed up … we had 627 students and didn't have to turn anyone away.

By this point, we had fourteen churches of various denominations in the county partnering with us to host this event. Each church donated money, time, and talent, despite our doctrinal differences, difference of opinions, and different personalities. The movement of camaraderie that God blessed our county with was unmatched. We worked through issues, lost our tempers, and forgave one another. Along with the powerful move of God to meld this group of varying denominations and opinions into one unit, this was the year we raised enough donations to provide pizza for everyone and to invite Thomas Young and Pierce to be our headliners. What a dream come true for Sarah, Angela, and our team.

That evening, every auditorium seat was filled. Thomas Young preached a message about how to accept Christ. He spent ten minutes explaining the gospel.

"All have sinned and fall short of the glory of God."
Romans 3:23 HCSB

"But God demonstrates His own love for us in this:
While we were still sinners,
Christ died for us."
Romans 5:8 NIV

"For God so loved the world, that He gave His only begotten Son,
that whosoever believeth in Him should not perish,
but have everlasting life."
John 3:16 KJV

"For He made Him who knew no sin to be sin for us, that we might
become the righteousness of God in Him."
2 Corinthians 5:21 NKJV

He told them Jesus loved them and that they could not earn their way to heaven. Trusting Jesus is the only way. Then, he spent twenty minutes trying to talk them out of making that decision. He challenged them by saying,

- **IF** you are not willing to sell your Nintendo and buy a pair of shoes for the boy whose sneakers has holes in them; and
- **IF** you are not willing to sit at lunch with unpopular or smelly kids; and

- **IF** you are not willing to bring your Bible to school and start a before or after school Bible study group,
- **THEN** you should not come forward.

When he finished speaking, the students moved to the altar in droves, tears streaming down the faces of boys and girls alike. Rich and poor, popular and unpopular they came. One hundred twenty-three students walked forward to accept Christ as their personal Savior. Twenty-five adult counselors were on standby, and what we thought would be one-on-one conversations or maybe one-on-two or one-on-three with each counselor, ended up being in groups of ten and fifteen.

When the event was over, Racquel and I debriefed. She wisely said, "We didn't pray big enough. If we had an even larger venue, God would have filled it up."

A Thousand Ways to Die in Arizona
Way #401: Toads

You read that right. Toads. There are toxic toads in Arizona. The Sonoran Desert toad lives underground most of the year but comes out to mate in late August and they literally invade like a plague! They excrete a poisonous toxin that can cause a rash but can cause severe illness or even death if ingested. I wouldn't go ingesting a frog, but I guess because it can cause a psychedelic experience, some people would. Gross.

Toads and frogs are very much alike; however, they are not the same. Toads have shorter legs and dry, warty skin. Conversely, frogs have smooth, slimy skin. Either way, we don't want frogs crawling all over our homes. The difference is real, but often unrecognized.

To the average person, the terms *toad* and *frog* are used interchangeably. This is important because it reminds us how Satan lies to us. He often uses the Word of God to tempt us to sin. He changes it just enough that we don't recognize the difference. Satan doesn't dispute the truth of the scriptures. Instead, he gives meaning to a passage that was never meant to be.

I stayed in a toxic marriage for 15 years, thinking divorce would be a sin against God. Satan used scripture against me to keep me locked into a relationship that was unhealthy and dangerous to me and my three children. Even the church was convinced I should stay in the toxic environment where poisons were being excreted day in and day out through the emotional and verbal abuse.

It took a few years for me and the kids to get settled into life and into our destiny, but we kept plugging along, making mistakes and getting back up again. No toxic toad was going to rob us of God's plan for our lives.

REFLECTION

1. How has God stretched your faith over the past few months? What have you learned through that stretching?

2. I talked about the miracle of feeding the hotdogs and the miracle of the weather. What miracles have you witnessed God perform on your behalf? If you can't think of any, ask God to open your spiritual eyes and ears so you can be more aware of His inner workings.

3. Read the scriptures Thomas Young used to share the gospel. Romans 3:23, Romans 5:8, John 3:16, 2 Corinthians 5:21. Which scripture resonates with you most today?

4. Look at the IF/THEN statements again. How would you respond?

- **IF** you are not willing to sell your Nintendo and buy a pair of shoes for the boy whose sneakers has holes in them; and
- **IF** you are not willing to sit at lunch with unpopular or smelly kids; and
- **IF** you are not willing to bring your Bible to school and start a before or after school Bible study group,
- **THEN** you should not come forward.

5. Are you praying BIG enough prayers? How can you pray bigger prayers? Add the outrageous, the unimaginable, the So Big Only God Could Do It. Write out your big, hairy, audacious prayer here:

6. I used the example of toads vs. frogs to share how the devil tricks us. Have you ever caught Satan trying to deceive you by confusing the truth of the Word with a similar but incorrect translation? How can you guard against this tactic?

CHAPTER

4

Beware

I belonged to the same church for over 23 years and did everything there except preach.[11] This church was home, and I loved being there. Having been raised Catholic, it was not unusual to go to church every day so after dropping the kids at school, I would often go there to pray. I even had my own key.

When I became frustrated or wanted to leave the church, God would say, "Grow where you are planted." Every. Single. Time. Until He didn't. I was upset with our pastor because I believed he was telling half-truths. One Sunday morning after hearing another half-truth that I knew to be incorrect, I prayed, "God, I can't do this anymore. Someone needs to leave; it's either me or him." After the service concluded, the pastor read his letter of resignation! I looked toward heaven and said, "Ok then."

On another occasion the Lord told me to beware of wolves in sheep's clothing. I didn't know at the time how prophetic those words were. Soon after, our church hired a new pastor who was exactly what God warned me about. After he had been there for a while, there was a direct assault on me involving that pastor, which caused the trauma from my childhood to surface. My panic attacks were so bad that I was unable to drive, and I felt so helpless and afraid that I left the church. I began having panic attacks and was unable to drive for a period as well as being a passenger in someone else's car. Forget elevators or stores with electronic doors. I recall being at a store with my son, Lance, and we weaved our way through the store. When I realized how far we were from the exit, I panicked. He put his arm around me and led me out of the store without condemnation. He was awesome but the experience was awful.

In the beginning, I didn't tell anyone. I had remarried, but I was afraid even to tell him. Then, the pastor emailed me, telling me to forget about what he said, trying to convince me that everything was fine. But I couldn't forget. I felt violated. I did not respond to his email. The following day, he sent another email threatening me. I called my best friend Racquel and through many tears I shared what had happened. She suggested I talk to the head deacon who called a meeting with the deacon board and their wives. I felt like I had support; like someone would believe me and help.

The next day, I received a third threatening email from the pastor, describing what would happen if I told anyone. I was afraid to tell my husband because I thought he would drive to the pastor's house and punch him in the face. So instead, I arranged for the two of us to go to Racquel's house. There, with Racquel and her husband present, I told my husband what had taken place. He was calm. Eerily calm. We explained that we had a meeting planned with the deacons and he agreed to be present.

My second husband had been a policeman for many years and had dealt with things like this and much worse. He knew how to stay calm and think through situations. I printed the emails and when the time came to meet with the deacons and their wives, through choked sobs, I told them what had taken place. The deacons agreed they would not use my name to the church body or yokefellows. The church leadership supported me, fired the pastor, and paid for me to see a Christian counselor who helped me immensely. But even though the pastor was fired, the church members (who were not given the names or particulars in order to protect me) argued over whether the pastor had done anything wrong. I knew he was a liar and a fraud so, unable to listen to people talk about him like he was innocent, I didn't return to the church.

I was starting to learn how God uses all circumstances to glorify Himself. Satan meant to bring me evil, but God turned it around!

Finding My Place to Belong

After surviving seven pastors and three building campaigns, it was time to leave the church, and I did not leave alone. A lot of people left; actually, most of them, and many started attending the same little church in a neighboring town. I joined them there along with my son and daughter-in-law, two of my grandbabies, and my neighbors, but it never felt like home. Partly because I was healing from the trauma I experienced at the last church and partly because I was in an unhappy marriage.

Marrying too quickly on the rebound from a long, abusive relationship was a bad idea. My new husband talked the talk. He knew Christian terms and he attended church with me, but he did not live out his faith during the week. I grew to resent him and was filled with guilt for having married him. In addition, I was caring for my special needs child, Destiny, who we adopted together from the foster care system. Her many doctor appointments, court hearings, and daily meltdowns took a lot of energy. In fact, I read that a "study found that stress hormones appeared at extremely low levels in mothers of Autistic children, levels similar to chronic stress situations, like soldiers in combat. These mothers have schedules that appear to be more stressful."[12] And that is how I felt. I was on alert 24/7 and seldom got an uninterrupted night's sleep. So, I went to church feeling self-conscious and awkward, like everyone was judging me, when in reality, I was judging myself.

> I was learning how God uses all circumstances to glorify Himself.

For seven years, even though I was in a Bible-teaching church and involved in prayer ministry, outreach/missions and other things, this new church never felt like home. I felt distant from God, like I just wasn't connecting.[13] I did grow spiritually, but not by leaps and bounds. I attended church on Sundays but couldn't wait to leave. I didn't want to talk to anyone, nor did I want to trust anyone. I was going through the motions but not engaging. I felt out of place, self-conscious, inferior, and defensive. Satan's attacks and lies led me to believe things that were not true.

I wasn't angry at God. I loved Him and leaned on Him. In fact, during this time I thought I was acting normally and everyone else was being weird. It wasn't until years later that I was able to see the truth. Satan had wormed his way into my relationships and was trying to take me out by using my trust issues from childhood and my first marriage. Then he used the hurt and loss that surfaced after the attack at church, filling me with more guilt and shame.

As foster parents, my husband and I continued to take in children who needed care. Our license was for a maximum of three children, so we often had sibling sets of three to keep them from being separated. We wanted to keep families together, but this added more stress, more court dates, more visitations with parents, more mental health appointments. Pouring into the lives of children and helping them overcome their own trauma was my outlet to ignore what needed to be addressed in my life. The years of abuse at the hands of my father, my first husband, and the pastor was piling on, and I buried my head in the sand. Advocating for the children in court and at school was a full time job, and it took its toll on my marriage and my mind. (I don't regret any of the help we provided, by the way.)

Eventually my husband and I realized we had irreconcilable differences. We tried marriage counseling, but it soon became apparent that things were not going to change. Destiny and I moved into an apartment in another town. With just the two of us, I could finally breathe and decided to fulfill a lifetime goal and return to college to earn my associate degree.[14] I enrolled in adult evening classes at MidAmerica Nazarene University.

Destiny and I joined a church near our home. It was pastored by my daughter Sarah's father-in-law, yet I had the same feelings of awkwardness, self-consciousness, and being out of my element. It didn't matter how many events I attended or how many teams I joined; something was missing. Still, I learned and grew.

In March 2019 the church announced a building project. They had outgrown their facility and purchased land across town in a high-traffic area with good visibility from the interstate where they would erect a new facility. Being a prayer warrior, I went to the new land to pray over it. While there, God told me I would not be part of the new church, which was not a surprise since I had never felt like I was part of the old church. Assuming He would send me to another church to check out, I waited for His direction.

A short time later, the associate pastor delivered a sermon called *Love Where You Are.*[15] He said, "Stay where you are until God tells you to move." I was in the middle of a lot of things. For example, I was deciding whether to continue my education and earn my bachelor's degree. Because of Covid, online classes looked good. I was renting a house, trying to decide whether to buy one. I was attending a church that I was not going to be part of. I was married but living separately.

So, when the pastor said, "Don't move until God says move," I thought, "Ok, I will stay in school, buy a house, attend this church, and stay married but separated." All the things. I will keep doing them until God tells me to move.

As a result, I did just that. I leaned into God, knowing I needed to draw nearer and listen to what He was saying. Covid had us homebound which made it easier to spend more time in the Bible. As I leaned into Him, I kept asking, *"What do You want me to do? I am here, I just don't know what You want me to do."*

I had prayed big prayers back with B2SB and seen God move in miracles, signs and wonders. Now in September 2020, He reminded me again to pray BIG prayers. Talk about God building my faith! He was showing me how powerful He is and how I can count on Him if I will only come to Him in prayer.

So, let's begin there.

A Thousand Ways to Die in Arizona
Way #332: Jaguars

While Jaguars are typically shy cats and prefer to avoid humans, they can and have been known to pounce when feeling threatened, surprised, or hungry. Unlike other big cats, they don't kill by suffocation. As an alternative, they use their unbelievably powerful jaw to penetrate through the skull of its prey. Jaguar is a Native American word meaning "he who kills with one blow."[10]

Five months after arriving in Arizona, the news reported a jaguar that had been roaming Arizona and Mexico for years had been spotted. El Jefe "The Boss" was back. Additionally, there were two other male jaguars in the area who were sleeping in caves or trees during the day. Do not explore caves when hiking. Noted.

Jaguars are opportunistic. They will prey on practically anything, seeking out the weak and vulnerable, pouncing with a fatal blow.

My father, like the jaguar, tried to kill Mama's spirit. And mine too, I suppose. He used his power as a respected business owner, member of the Elks Club, and member of the Catholic church to powerfully hold us in his grip. But like jaguar, he also avoided any real human interaction that he wasn't in control of. When Mama got bold and stood her ground, he finally slunk away.

The "wolf in sheep's clothing" pastor saw me as broken and weak, and he directly assaulted me. His actions caused my childhood trauma to surface, resulting in panic and anxiety, and pushing me into the jaws of helplessness and fear.

REFLECTION

1. I shared that I didn't feel like the church I was attending was home. I also shared that I didn't engage and was just going through the motions. How would engaging have helped me feel more accepted?

2. Have you ever avoided human interaction and been in a mindset to sit back and wait for others to welcome you to a new church rather than jumping in and welcoming others? If so, what difference did it make? If not, what difference would that make?

3. What do you look for in a church home? How can you bring those same things into the church you attend?

4. The pastor said, "Stay where you are until God tells you to move." Do you find it difficult to wait on God when you are ready to go?

5. Satan is ready to pounce and is seeking whom he can devour. Did you pray a BIG prayer today? What are you waiting for?

6. Read Hebrews 10:24-25. Think about how you can encourage someone in their faith today. Write down the name of the person you thought of and pray about what to do and how it will be received. Come back later and make a note about the outcome. Thank God for the opportunity to do good works. If you are not part of a church yet, write down the name of one you will commit to visit this week.

5

Twelve Hundred Miles

I prayed a big prayer. "Lord, what do You want me to do?" He answered in a big way. But was it an answer I was ready or willing to hear?

The Big Answer | Clue #1

Due to several health issues related to cold weather, my doctor suggested I move from Kansas to Arizona. Have you heard of Raynaud's Syndrome? According to the Mayo Clinic, it typically happens to people who live in cold climates and is not completely understood. From personal experience I know that it turns my fingers white (or blue, or bright red) when cold or stressed. It can also happen in my toes, ear lobes, nose, or lips. Raynaud's hurts! It causes a sensation of pins and needles that can be overwhelmingly painful. Naturally, I have Raynaud's.

I didn't think much of the doctor's suggestion because I had no intention of moving away from my children and grandchildren. That wasn't an option. The following year, a different doctor, a slight woman in her mid-thirties, began sharing the health benefits of moving to a warmer climate, perhaps Arizona. As I sat on the exam room table politely listening, I was thinking to myself, "Yes, I understand I may be more comfortable in a warmer climate. But no, I don't have any intention of leaving my children and grandchildren, thank you very much." Besides, I was steeped deeply into my community. I was also a foster mom of 58 kids who had come through the system. I wasn't moving anywhere. Then I added, "Unless God tells me to."

Of all the warm weather states in America, why did they both suggest Arizona? It seemed like coincidence, but I don't believe in coincidence. I believe in the power of God.

Shortly after, I reconnected with a few friends from junior high school through social media.[16] One of those friends was Billy Todd. He was thrilled to hear from me and recounted the hilarious stories of having a crush on me while I didn't know he was even alive. He laughed about how one time I said hello to him in the hallway and he literally walked face first into the wall of lockers. He was good at retelling stories in a fascinating, entertaining way. Then he started inviting me to visit him in Arizona. I hadn't seen him in over 40 years, so his invitation made me laugh because it seemed so absurd. It seemed ludicrous, but back in our school days, he could always make me laugh too. That was mostly what I remembered about him – his fun loving personality.

Over the next several weeks he asked me several times to consider visiting, suggesting I might like it enough to move there! Arizona seemed to be pursuing me, first through the words of two doctors and then through an old school friend.

The Big Answer | Clue #2

One Sunday morning, I got up early as usual. I am a morning person; I wake up happy. Not surprisingly, I enjoy attending the first service of the day. Our church holds three services, one right after the other and the first one is always my favorite. So, I arrived at church early and parked in the adjoining elementary school parking lot used for overflow parking. Walking across the street toward the church, I took in the beige exterior and dark brown roof of the square shaped building. Greeters were smiling and holding open the double glass doors as people approached. I turned my head to read the sign in the parking lot proclaiming, "We are glad you are here!"

As I crossed the threshold into the building, I was welcomed by a huge banner on the wall. It was bright red and in large white letters had one single word, "MOVE." I stood there in awe and said to God, "Wow. You sent me a literal sign." As I walked down the hallway there were two large banners with bright red letters that seemed to be waving at me. Their message bore into my heart, "Move. Move."

> It seemed God was determined to pluck me from my comfort zone and prepare me for a new ministry field.

As I made my way into the sanctuary I took in the sights and sounds. Our worship center was actually a gymnasium with rows of padded chairs that link together to form pews. The podium was on a makeshift wooden stage painted black and in the center was a tall brown podium with a Bible laid open to the passage of the day. A row of chairs was set up against the back wall, designed for parents with young children who may need to exit during the service. When I first started attending church, my daughter had three little children, so I sat with her. Then sitting there became a habit. As I found my seat, I looked up at the pulpit. Behind the stage was a digital image of the word "Move." It seemed the month of October 2021 was when God determined to pluck me from my comfort zone and prepare me for a new ministry field.

The Big Answer | Clue #3

Pastor Rick, a tall thin man of about sixty, wearing sneakers, blue jeans, and a t-shirt, stepped forward to welcome everyone. After a few dad jokes, he began to preach his sermon titled, *Prepare to Move.* His opening question was, "Are you ready to move?" He was referring to being active in the church rather than sitting on the sidelines. He encouraged the congregation to recognize there were ministries where they were gifted to serve and to listen to what the Holy Spirit was saying about getting involved.

Everything he said resonated and convicted me that God did, in fact, want me to move from Kansas to Arizona. As he preached my smile faded. I realized that long ago, I promised God I would go wherever He sends, and I knew He was about to send me.

China. That's where I assumed God would send me. Or Mexico. Somewhere that frightened me. But Arizona? That was not what I expected.

From Pastor Lucas' sermon two years earlier, I heard "Stay where you are until God says to move!" Now with Pastor Rick's sermon, I was hearing, "Move!" I had complete surety that God was speaking, and I may not have known what He was doing but I knew for certain that He was speaking to me.

The following week, as we moved into our new home, I pondered so many things. I was excited to be a homeowner again, to have my own place. I knew Mama would be proud of me. I was in the middle of ordering new furniture, rugs, and décor while also making plans to put in a fence for my dogs and order a load of gravel for the driveway.

I recall that even as I ordered rugs and blinds and furniture, I could feel a gnawing in the back of my mind. As if the sap of a pencil cacti had dried on my skin, I was feeling a burning in my heart and irritation in my spirit. Why would God NOT want me to make my new home livable? It didn't make sense. That's why I ignored the still small voice that warned me not to make these purchases.

I had been separated for more than three years, but neither of us had filed for a divorce. Around the same time, Destiny wanted to attend Kansas State University to become a veterinarian, and with college comes student loans, FAFSA forms, and proving income. My husband and I filed our tax forms as a married couple, but I was living on my own income and needed the financial help for Destiny's education, so I filed for divorce. We had no minor children and all our assets had been liquidated and divided, so the divorce was over and done in a matter of weeks.

My now ex-husband and I were amicable for the sake of our family. He was still the only grandpa the grandkids knew, and I did not want to take that away from them, and he was Destiny's father. I also pondered taking Destiny away from her father and the challenges moving to Arizona would cause, but much like the hardy pencil cactus that can grow just about anywhere and flourish, children tend to grow into the role they need as the only way to survive. So, I did what I could to help them cultivate and maintain a loving relationship. That would take some time. In the meantime, God was talking to me, and I was listening. The excitement of owning my own home and readying it for my life as an empty nester seemed like it was going to be short-lived.

The Big Answer | Clue #4

On a subsequent Sunday, all three church services were combined into one. The church family met together at our new location to pray and worship as one body of believers. From an outdoor stage built on our new land, Pastor Rick preached a sermon titled, *Move from Here to There*, saying "move forward with faith!" The ground was rough and full of dirt clods, making walking precarious; yet it was amazing to see lawn chairs in a vacant field off the interstate, hands and voices raised to God in worship. Then he said, "Faith is the willingness to move on a maybe. Where is God calling you?"

I knew where God was calling me, and I was not ready to surrender to it. Then the pastor asked everyone to come forward and receive a free gift. I made my way up the dusty path, winding through the uneven rows of the crude church pews, to the front of the stage. There I was handed a dog-tag type necklace with one word engraved on it "MOVE." It also had an arrow etched through the word.

We were instructed to take the necklace home and hang it somewhere visible as a reminder of what God was saying. I did not want to be reminded. I stuck mine in the back corner of a dresser in my closet. I joked with my friend about all the signs to move, but in my heart it wasn't funny. I was terrified of the future. And to be afraid of the future was something I had been familiar with since I was a child, hoping my father wouldn't come home.

The Big Answer | Clue #5

The next week, Pastor Rick preached a sermon titled, *From Comfort Zone to Danger Zone*.[17] "Anytime God is calling you to do something, people are going to spread a bad report about you. God is bigger than the obstacles. Quit holding on to what's holding you back. Excuses are self-imposed limitations." Like the hardy pencil cactus that just won't die, the pastor's message was being hammered into me, unbeknownst to him. I thought, "Ok God, I hear you, but I don't like what You are saying."

I don't know if people were spreading a bad report about me, but I know they were talking about me. They thought I was crazy not only for moving 1,200 miles away, but also for saying God told me He wanted me to move. I would walk into a room, and everyone would go silent and not make eye contact with me. That was a good indication there was talk going on behind my back. I wasn't surprised because Pastor Rick had prepared me.

The ridicule made me think about Noah.[18] It had never rained before, yet he was building a giant ark. I know people must have thought he was crazy; they didn't know what rain, or a flood was. He spent years building the big boat, enduring ridicule for a long time, and he kept moving forward.

I had to keep moving forward, too, and not listen to the naysayers.

All the while, the days from one Sunday to the next, I was in prayer and in the Word. Also, I was talking to Billy Todd frequently. We were getting to know each other and had become great friends. The one thing I didn't really share with him was the seriousness of me moving to Arizona. Not for him, but for God. It was great that he was there, but even if he wasn't, I knew God was calling me to Arizona.

Somewhere in the middle of this sermon series, church members were asked to pray about making a commitment for the Move building campaign. Everyone who turned in a card received a t-shirt. When I received my shirt, it was rolled up and tied with a burlap string. I didn't bother to unwrap it; I was busy unpacking things at home, so I put it in one of my piles, alongside the dog-tag necklace with the word "Move" inscribed on it.

A Thousand Ways to Die in Arizona
Way #624: Pencil Cacti

The sap from this cactus is poisonous. If you are allergic to latex, and of course I am, it may cause seizures, coma, and even death! Learn how to spot one immediately. Done!

The sap from the pencil cacti is much like that of a fig tree. Both are pasty, white sap and are poisonous to animals and humans. It can cause a rash, burning, and even blindness. Unlike the fig tree's sap, though, that from a pencil cactus (for those who are also allergic to latex), could in rare cases, cause death. Oppositely, it has been used in accepted treatments in some cultures to cure cancer and other tumors. Known for being resilient and able to thrive in tough conditions, both plants symbolize power and stamina.

The Bible does not specifically speak about cactus; it does mention barren ground with bad water in 2 Kings 2:19 New Century Version. "*The people of the city said to Elisha, 'Look, master, this city is a nice place to live as you can see. But the water is so bad the land cannot grow crops.*" Sounds like Arizona to me!

Like the pencil cactus, we need to be resilient and able to thrive in tough conditions. God is with us wherever we go (Psalm 139: 9-10). Some things that may appear harmful or detrimental, or perhaps we simply don't understand what God is doing, can end up being the very thing that saves our life. Never doubt that God is always in control, and He has a good plan (1 Peter 5:6-7).

REFLECTION

1. Do you believe in coincidences, or do you see them as the power of God? Journal your insights.

2. When God speaks sometimes it takes a while for us to realize it's His orchestration and not mere happenstance. In your 20/20 hindsight vision, what has God orchestrated in your life that took you a while to recognize or realize? Explain.

3. Do you know someone who may be a good person but is not a born again Christian. Maybe it's you? How can you know the difference?

4. Have you tried to ignore God's voice when He's asked you to do something you didn't want to do? Journal your answer below.

5. Like the pencil cacti we need to be resilient. "Excuses are self-imposed limitations." Do you agree? Why or why not?

6. Read Psalm 139:9-10 and 1 Peter 5:6-7. How do these verses encourage you in God's love, guidance, and provision? Do they remind you that God is in control?

6

From Interest to Impact

The Big Answer | Clue 6

T he next week's sermon was *From Interest to Impact.* The pastor said, "Be faithful and obedient to what God calls you to do. God is preparing to throw something your way. Out of nowhere will come a calling. Something, a big assignment, a new call, is coming. When God tells us to do something, we're going to do it until He tells us not to do it anymore." My eyes were filled with tears, my heart was filled with conviction, and my brain was filled with fear. I asked, "How God? Why?"

The conviction in my heart knew God was calling me even though I couldn't admit it. I had closed on my house and had a mortgage. I couldn't afford to move or to rent somewhere else. I had kids and grandkids, and I didn't want to leave them. It was mind-boggling. And besides, everyone would think I was crazy, and I cared about that. Then, the Holy Spirit spoke to my spirit, *"You are not where God wants you to be.... yet."*

I was fairly certain God was calling me to move to Arizona. But as of yet, I didn't know why He would ask such a hard thing. Twelve hundred miles is a two-day drive away from my kids, my grandkids, my new house and friends, everything I knew and everything familiar.

The last day of October 2020, I wrote in my prayer journal, "You are not where God wants you to be… yet." The following Sunday, the pastor said, "Move from where you are to where God wants you to be," I was overwhelmed. I know people hear God differently. He speaks through our circumstances, prayer, His Word, and other people. He was speaking to me in all these ways. He says in John 10:27, *"My sheep hear My voice, I know them, and they follow Me."* I knew His voice and I was following. I pondered all of this in my heart, devouring the Bible and steeped in prayer.

As October morphed into November and then December, Arizona kept beckoning, and the word "move" continued to be in my face. Once the *Move* sermon series was completed in October, I assumed the banners, table covers, and displays would come down. I was taken aback when, walking into the annual women's ornament exchange the first weekend in December, I saw the theme was "Move." The tables were gaily decorated with festive colors and the word "MOVE" was splayed across the table like a banner, daring anyone to contradict its message.

> I journaled these things so when Satan tried to twist things and confuse me, I could go back and recall plainly what God said and not be fooled by the enemy's tactics.

After much inner turmoil and conflict, I found myself sitting in my parked car in my gravel driveway, engine running, listening to Christian music. Feeling the need to surrender, I turned the volume down and prayed.

"God, if this is really You telling me to move to Arizona, and if I am not just a crazy person who thinks you are saying that, then I know you won't move me without a ministry. So could you at least tell me what that is?"

As if lightning struck, I was shaken when immediately the radio personality announced an interview with Gary Webb of OCJ Kids Ministry in Phoenix, Arizona! I turned up the volume and listened to the interview. Gary had founded OCJ Kids to mentor and aid foster kids aging out of the system. Remember, I am the foster mom of 58 kids, so I sat there dumbfounded, in complete awe of God. He gave me a ministry close to my heart!

Perhaps you have heard the saying, "I threw out my fleece." Fleece is a piece of wool. When I asked God to tell me what my ministry was, I threw out my fleece, so to speak. But I was not alone in seeking God's confirmation. A hero of faith did the same thing.

"Then Gideon said to God, 'If You will deliver Israel by my hand as you said I will put a fleece of wool here on the threshing floor. If dew is only on the fleece, and all the ground is dry, I will know that You will deliver Israel by my strength, as You said.' And that is what happened. When he got up early in the morning, he squeezed the fleece and wrung dew out of it, filling a bowl with water. Gideon then said to God, 'Don't be angry with me; let me speak one more time. Please allow me to make one more test with the fleece. Let it remain dry, and the dew be all over the ground.' That night God did as Gideon requested: only the fleece was dry, and dew was all over the ground."
Judges 6:36-40 HCSB

The next morning as I woke up, I threw out another fleece. "Lord, you know if this is really, *really* You, I need to see that word, 'move' one more time."

I opened social media and the first post I saw said, "Don't make an assumption that you have more time. Move as if you don't." That's all I needed. I tipped my head back, looked at the ceiling and prayed, "I hear You loud and clear." He clearly said GO.

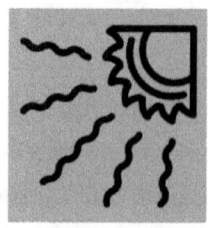

A Thousand Ways to Die in Arizona
Way #571: Heat

Summer 2022 was Arizona's deadliest on record for heat-related fatalities. With temperatures up to 120 degrees and a growing homeless population, it was not unexpected. Never leave people in the car without the air conditioning running, and don't plan outdoor activities in the heat of the day. It's reverse winter in Arizona. Plan accordingly.

Dear Reader,

The story really could stop here. God clearly said go and yet, human that I am, there are many more times of doubt between then and now. What has helped me to have faith and remember what God has said, the miraculous ways He has spoken to me, is I journal. I write these things down because when Satan tries to twist things and confuse me, I go back to what I've written and recall plainly what God has said. This guards me from being pulled into the enemy's tactics.

I have a prayer journal, and I encourage you to have one, too. It doesn't have to be fancy; a legal pad or composition notebook will work just fine – whatever you have or can afford. Just do it. It's helpful to go back and read all the goodness God has done for you. If you don't write it, you'll forget. Don't allow Satan to frustrate you. If you've written things down, you can recall them plainly and will not be fooled by his tactics to mislead you.

REFLECTION

1. After six clues, I was finally ready to accept God's call, but I still asked why. Can you relate? Do you want or need all the answers before committing or moving in obedience?

2. Are you where God wants you to be? Are you confident you are in alignment with His plan and will?

3. John 10:27 says, *"My sheep hear My voice, I know them, and they follow me."* Do you hear the Shepherd's voice? What are you doing to fine tune His voice in your heart and spirit?

4. Have you ever laid a fleece before the Lord as Gideon did in Judges 6:36-40? What was the result?

5. Did you obey what God showed you in answer to your fleece?

6. Start a prayer journal and write about the goodness of God in your life to help you remember. Don't allow Satan to frustrate you by telling you that God has not worked on your behalf.

CHAPTER

7

Pray Big Prayers

I recalled Raquel's statement after the big B2BS event, "We didn't pray big enough. If we had had a larger venue, God would have filled it up."

The day after hearing God say He wanted me to move to Arizona, I made plans to visit Raquel who was now living in Albuquerque, New Mexico. This was December 14, 2021. My life was in an upheaval of not knowing what was happening, and I wanted to share with her all the things God was doing and the direction He was leading. She was off work from Thursday through Sunday, and my job was portable, so off I went.

My twelve hour drive to her house was spent mostly in silence. My phone battery would not hold a charge, and my old-fashioned cigarette lighter charging station wasn't working properly. I didn't want to get stuck on a desert highway without a working phone, so I sat the phone aside. Driving through Oklahoma and Texas offered me the choice of listening to country music, which isn't my favorite, and as I got closer to New Mexico, the radio turned to static, so I drove in silence. This afforded me the chance to think and to give God a chance to remind me to pray BIG prayers.

After arriving at Raquels, I lay in bed one morning and opened my Bible study called *Advent: The Journey to Christmas. A Church of the Highlands Devotional.* On day 19, I read:

"Think of a time when you heard from God, whether it was a promise, a confirmation, or a conviction. What was your immediate response? Did you act on what He said, or did you sit and ponder whether it was really His voice? Maybe you were sure you heard what He said, but still hesitated."[19]

The key verse was Luke 2:15-20.

"When the angels had left them and returned to heaven, the shepherds said to one another, 'Let's go straight to Bethlehem and see what has happened, which the Lord has made known to us.' They hurried off and found both Mary and Joseph, and the baby who was lying in the feeding trough. After seeing them, they reported the message they were told about this child, and all who heard it were amazed at what the shepherds said to them. But Mary was treasuring up all these things in her heart and meditating on them. The shepherds returned, glorifying and praising God for all they had seen and heard, just as they had been told." (HCSB)

The devotional talked about how the shepherds hurried off to find Jesus after the angels gave them the Good News about his birth. They didn't hesitate nor did they question the message they had received. Their faith moved them forward. They didn't worry about who would watch their sheep, whether they were dressed appropriately to meet a king, or whether to tell anyone else what they had heard. They immediately responded to God.

Then, it challenged me to embrace a faith that doesn't hesitate because that creates a breeding ground for doubt, fear, and insecurity, which comes from the enemy. We are to trust His direction, knowing He will equip us to do what He's asked. All He wants is our yes.

The devotional closed with a prayer asking God for His patience, forgiveness, and strength to respond immediately when He speaks. It ended with Proverbs 3:5-6:

> *"Trust in the Lord with all your heart, and do not rely on your own understanding; think about Him in all your ways, and He will guide you on the right paths."* (HCSB)

Those were the words I needed to hear that morning. My original plan was to wait until after the Christmas holidays to visit OCJ Kids. I had written the date for the visit on my timeline – January 7, 2022. But it seemed on this day, God had another plan in mind. I woke Racquel to read the devotional. All she could say was, "Wow." I replied, "Yeah, I gotta go."

Within 30 minutes, I was dressed, packed, and ready for the six hour drive to OCJ Kids in Phoenix, Arizona.

A Thousand Ways to Die in Arizona
Way #817: Oleander

The oleander shrub enjoys the hot dry climate of Arizona and grows easily throughout the state. Its carefree habit and distinguished pink flowers make it a favorite for landscaping. Sometimes used in medicine for cardiac arrest and diabetes among others, some folks have tried to self-medicate by consuming oleander tea. This can cause numbness and swelling of the mouth and tongue, immediate nausea and diarrhea, and may lead to death. More commonly, young children and pets are at risk of putting the leaves in their mouths. Note to self: identify the plants in the yard.

Oleander is a poisonous plant that appears as a beautiful flowering bush. Many in Arizona use it in their yards for decoration.

Sometimes people or situations can appear desirable, but we need to use wisdom and caution when planting people or things into our lives. Praying big prayers ensures God's best for us and doesn't limit the flowering to be pretty on the outside but toxic on the inside.

REFLECTION

1. Who is in your circle of friends that helps you cultivate the flowering process of God's work and activity in your life? Be sure to pray for them and thank them.

2. When God speaks, do you respond immediately, or do you hesitate? Is delayed obedience the same as obedience, or is it disobedience?

3. Deuteronomy 29:18 *"Be sure there is no man, woman, clan, or tribe among you today whose heart turns away from the Lord our God to go and worship the gods of those nations. Be sure there is no root among you bearing poisonous and bitter fruit."* What do you think it means to "bear poisonous fruit"?

4. 4. Matthew 7:17 *"Likewise, every good tree bears good fruit, but a bad tree bears bad fruit."* The fruit you bear are the deeds you do, the words you say, the actions you take. Are you bearing more good fruit than bad fruit? Is that enough? What changes can you make to ensure you are a good tree?

5. Do you agree with this statement:
   "Hesitation creates a breeding ground for doubt, fear, and insecurity."
   Why or why not?

6. 6. Read Proverbs 3:5-6. How does this scripture speak to you today?

8

Stepping into the Call

P ulling slowly into the parking lot, the OCJ Kids building looked more like a storage facility than an office building. I was legitimately concerned that I had gone to the wrong location as I surveyed the silver garage doors lined one after the other. I tried calling to confirm I was in the right location, but voicemail picked up. Disappointment turned to relief as I drove to the other side of the building and saw a storefront with doors and windows. Then I saw the sign that read "CLOSED."

Regardless, I parked my car and got out to tug on the entrance door in hopes that someone was inside. Seeing a light in the back hallway, I pounded on the windows. Not getting a response, I texted Racquel that no one was there, and I didn't know what to do. Then I asked God, "Do you want me to wait or…" At that moment, a blue SUV pulled into the parking lot and parked, leaving one space between us. Looking at me warily, a middle-aged woman stepped out of the vehicle. Her long brown hair was graying at the temples but her skin glowed, belying her age. I moved toward her and asked, "Are you with OCJ Ministries?" Her blue-gray eyes squinted slightly as she answered guardedly, "Yes, but we are closed for the holidays and will not reopen for ten more days."

I responded, "I know," then added, "I don't know what you have been praying for, but God just sent me 1,200 miles to be here, so here I am!" My knees were liquid. I wanted to either hug her neck and cry or fall prostrate on the ground and worship, but standing up was not one of the options I was considering. She didn't seem inclined to hug me as she answered, "Well, come on in and I'll show you around." I was grateful she allowed the Holy Spirit to interrupt her day, her plans, and her agenda, even though I could tell she didn't feel an immediate connection with me.

The woman graciously gave me a tour of the facility, including the library, warehouse, which explained the rolling garage doors on the back of the building, and offices. She shared information about the seventeen ministries managed through their organization. She showed me a shelf stocked with suitcases containing an inflatable mattress and air pump, bedding, pillow, toiletries, etc. Then she told me about their budget and staff. It was a thorough look inside the operation.

When the tour was complete, she leaned against the counter, looked at me intently and asked, "So, are you ready to move?" Her words caught me off guard as I remembered those were the first words Pastor Rick said in his sermon series that started this whole adventure. The commitment t-shirt I was given had made its way into my suitcase. Being in a hurry that morning, I unrolled it, pulled it on over my head, and was surprised to see the imprint on the front, "Ready to Move." It was clear God was using yet another person to confirm my call to relocate to Arizona.

During the six hour drive back to Racquel, I contemplated all God had done. Then, once I had comfortably settled back into her brown overstuffed sofa, she and I went over everything that had transpired that day. Wisely, she insisted I make a timeline saying, "You're going to forget what is happening." We used a timeline during the Back 2 Skool Bash, which had been helpful, so I started a timeline and daily wrote the things God was revealing.

With everything going in my heart, I knew it was time to tell my kids what was happening in my spiritual walk and my thought process, but I was nervous how they would respond. I wanted to explain how I had reconnected with Billy Todd who lived in Arizona, and I was being called to Arizona, but that one thing had nothing to do with the other. I knew it would look that way to outsiders.

I talked with them one on one, and each of their responses shocked me while also making me proud. My second son, Lance, lives in Hawai'i, so I knew the move wouldn't impact him much and I was right. He was full of support, encouragement, and excitement, giving me his blessing. "Go for it, Mom. Do what makes you happy."

My youngest child, Destiny, who doesn't handle change well also gave me a thumbs up. She said, "Go Mama. It's time for you to be happy." She didn't want to move with me because she had a boyfriend and a job she enjoyed, assuring me she would be fine.

My daughter Sarah and I had been close since her childhood years. Out of high school, she attended MidAmerica Nazarene University and earned her degree in family counseling. She was married with three children of her own. When I told her about my calling, with kindness and wisdom she said, "Mom, as a child I want you to stay here. I want you to choose me. But as a parent, I know you can do everything for your kids and become a shell of yourself. I don't want you to be a shell. Go be a person." I don't know if she learned that in her education but those were the sweetest, kindest, and wisest words she could have spoken.

Finally, I talked with my son, Eric, on New Year's Eve. After explaining how God was leading, he looked at me with sincerity and said,

"Mom, I'm going to tell you a story.

"I woke up one day and God said to me, 'Go read to somebody in a nursing home.' I asked, 'What? That's a strange thing to think.' I shoved it out of my brain, but it kept coming back over the next few days. Finally, I asked my wife, Yvonne, 'Who do we know that lives in a nursing home?' She mentioned a woman from our former church, so I called the woman's adult son who also attended church with us. I said, 'I need to come read to your mom.' We made a plan to go read and the date didn't work, so we rescheduled it. When the new date came around, something came up again and we had to reschedule again. Her son said, 'You know Eric, you don't have to do this.' I responded, 'No, you don't understand, I *do* have to do this!'

"We scheduled another date which finally worked out. We went and visited her in the nursing home, and I read Scripture to her. I read different Scriptures and then I turned to Isaiah 49:15 and read, '...*even if these forget, yet I will not forget you.*' This frail woman suffering from Spina bifida and curled into herself began to cry. She lifted her thin, aged hand and pointed at her Bible across the room. She said, 'You see my Bible over there by the T.V.? I haven't opened it in a week because I thought God had forgotten about me.'

"The date we were there was her late husband's birthday which made the visit extra special and comforted her. She was reminded that she was not forgotten, and it gave her strength.

"I tell you this story, Mom, to say, you've got to do what God says."

My children blessed me and sent me off, confirming to me, yet again, that God was in the move, and I was following where He was leading.

That same day, Billy Todd called with a question. "What time is the service at your church?" Confused, I responded, "We don't have church on New Year's Eve. What are you talking about?" Equally confused he claimed in a like tone, "We *always* have church on New Year's Eve! What are *you* talking about?" Shrugging my shoulders in surrender I inquired what church he went to. He gave me the church name, Pilgrim Rest Baptist Church, and I committed to watch the service online.

A Thousand Ways to Die in Arizona
Way #399: Crushed by a Cacti

Saguaro cacti can weigh over two tons when fully hydrated. With a root system that is only a few inches deep, they can fall in high winds or in dry spells that shrivel the roots. Don't rest in the shadow of one of these native beasts. Noted.

Unwilling to allow my spirit to be crushed, I went ahead and tugged on all the doors at OCJ. I knew God had led me to Arizona and I wanted to make sure to give Him every opportunity to show me why I was there.

REFLECTION

1. Have you ever jumped to the conclusion of what God might be doing only to find out you jumped too soon? Explain.

2. Are you ready to move into what God has for you? Why do you hesitate? How can you overcome your fear?

3. When God reveals something to us, that's an intimate moment between us and God. Do you keep a journal detailing these encounters? You should!

4. Who encourages your obedience to God? Someone who doesn't ridicule or second guess what you are hearing? If you don't have anyone, ask God to bring that someone to you.

5. Does this story convict your heart and faith in any way? If so, how?

6. What is trying to crush your spirit or your dreams today? How can you overcome the heaviness of the oppressor and move forward in obedience?

CHAPTER

9

Get Ready

The woman I met from OCJ Kids shared with me that one of their full-time staff members was leaving once she passed her state nursing exam, and they would need to fill the opening. Shortly afterward, God laid on my heart to start preparing. I felt led to update my resume. Was this what God wanted me to do or was I using human logic to solve the puzzle of why He was moving me to Arizona? Like putting a jigsaw puzzle together without all the pieces and without the top of the box that shows what it should look like upon completion. I knew I would need a job in Arizona if I made the move, and I thought maybe this was God's answer to my financial provision.

That New Year's Eve, my 14-year-old foster daughter and I decided to create our vision boards. She had been in and out of foster homes, and her behavior reflected the trouble and trauma that comes from feeling not wanted or loved.

Creating vision boards was a tradition for me, but it was new to her. To help her with ideas, I asked questions, "If you could do anything in the world, what would it be? Nothing is too outlandish!" I asked, "Where do you hope to be in five years? What do you want your life to look like?" As we narrowed down her answers, we spread out the poster boards and tape, glue guns and glitter, magazines, and colorful markers. Then we cut out pictures from magazines that gave her ideas. It was fun watching her get excited and to watch her overcome the fear of doing something wrong or being judged. She tilted her vision board "Make 22 Great." Then she listed things that would make it great: get a job, a driving permit, a support dog, earn straight As on her report card, learn photography, create a TikTok video about being in the foster system to make it a safe place for other kids. My heart rejoiced at how she wanted to grow and achieve great things.

My vision board was labeled "Forward." I added things about the potential move, the desert, and OCJ Kids.

At 10 p.m., I tuned into the Pilgrim Rest Baptist Church Watch Night,[20] located in Phoenix, Arizona. On Saturday, January 1, 2022, God confirmed my vision board words, FORWARD and MOVE, using my YouVersion app, which said, "God always has a way forward. You just have to keep moving." How powerful and intimate He is![21]

On Sunday, January 2, from my home in Kansas, I once again tuned into the Pilgrim Rest Baptist Church (PRBC) Sunday morning service. The sermon title was *How to Get a Prayer Through in 2022*. Rev. Dr. Terry E. Mackey, Jr. reminded me to always praise God, to put Him first, and then he asked,

"Are you ready to go higher?" He continued, "God's going to blow your mind. Hang in there, the best is yet to come! He is going to make it worth your time. The blessing will be doubled. Today is the first day of the best days of your life." Then he said, "It's not an accident that you're here." I was thinking, "No, it's not an accident. There are no coincidences with God."

I knew I was there for a reason,[22] and I was encouraged that God was going to see this through. The messages over the past three days from this church resonated with me, and I knew this was my new church home. I hadn't felt that in over ten years. "Lord, I don't understand how I can feel so at home and connected to this body of believers 1,200 miles away." The overwhelming feeling of emotions coupled with the physical fullness in my chest was almost more than I could take. I bowed and released the emotions with many tears.

Then Dr. Mackey said, "If we strive inward, upward, and outward, we move forward!" It was only the second day of the year and again I heard those two words from my vision board: move forward.

He explained that to strive inward is to keep it real. We are to be authentic, genuine, and real with ourselves, not harboring sin but confessing it to God. He referenced Psalm 66:18 and 1 John 1:9. Confessing our sin keeps our relationship with God open so He will hear us.

He told how striving outward is to keep it real with others. We need to stay humble, and we need God. He added, "It isn't a coincidence God is calling you." Then, I heard the Lord whisper to my heart that I was to start a YouTube channel. I wasn't ready for that, but I knew He was preparing me so my mind would be open when the time was right.

That same day at NLCC in Kansas, the pastor quoted Joshua 1:9. *"Haven't I commanded you; be bold and courageous? Do not be afraid or discouraged, for the Lord your God is with you wherever you go."* This, too, gave me the confidence to keep moving in the direction God was leading.

God didn't stop there! Later that day, I saw a message from Pastor Andy Addis titled, *The Direction of Forward.*[23,24] Pastor Andy had been the speaker at the Back 2 Skool Bash all those years ago. Because of the title and who was preaching it, I was certain I needed to listen. He preached from Deuteronomy 7:17-19 and talked about our mindset, our vision, and how to see what God has put before us. He said, "The inner me becomes the enemy because the inner me has the voice of the enemy." He went on to say that faith is all about the trajectory. God gives us the direction to go and when He gives the direction, we are to go.

Through his wisdom, Pastor Andy mentioned that we sometimes pick out verses in the Bible and try to make them say what we want them to say, but he reminded me that what is said in the Old Testament is echoed in the New Testament. Deuteronomy 7:19 was spoken to the Israelites who had wandered the desert for 40 years and when the time came to enter the Promised Land, they were rethinking their capability. This verse was to remind them of what God had done in the past and to encourage them to build on that trust and not be afraid. He explained that the word "remember" in the original text was emphatic and meant to always remember and never forget.

He then mentioned scripture found in Mark 11:1-3.

> *"Now when they drew near Jerusalem, to Bethphage and Bethany, at the Mount of Olives, He sent two of His disciples; and He said to them, 'Go into the village opposite you; and as soon as you have entered it, you will find a colt tied, on which no one has sat. Loose it and bring it. And if anyone says to you, "Why are you doing this?" say, "The Lord has need of it," and immediately he will send it here."* NKJV

Pastor Andy added, "You might recall from Matthew 21:1-7 that it was a young colt still with its mama which is why it had not been sat upon."

He explained that the animal equivalent to stubborn is a donkey and he shed light that the stubborn beast tied up was released in the name of Jesus. He personalized it and said, "If Jesus can do that for a donkey, He can certainly do that for us. So, if you're stuck in your present circumstances, remember the past. Remember what God has done. Stop being afraid. Instead of focusing on fear, focus on the things God has done in the past. Always remember and never forget."[25]

He then moved to Acts 4:31 which tells us that they were filled with the Holy Spirit, and they moved forward. This cemented the calling God was pushing me toward. It was imperative that I keep my eyes on what was before me rather than focusing on what I was moving away from. Following God meant moving forward. I knew what He was speaking into my heart, there was no denying it, and I was writing it down so I wouldn't forget.

Pastor Andy highlighted these things, too:

> Take a step. God's plan for our future is better than our own.
> Confess our sins which is agreeing with God that
> something is sin.

Repent if we have sin in our life.

Submit to God's leading.

Trust where God is taking us.

The final sermon I heard on January 2, 2022, was from Rev. Kenneth Martin from Greater Archview Baptist Church in Little Rock, Arkansas.[26] This pastor was in Little Rock but was from my hometown. I went to school with his brothers and listened to him on Sundays. This sermon was PUSH, Pray Until Something Happens. He referenced Daniel 6 when the King ordered everyone to bow down to him and pray only to him. Daniel kept praying, as was his habit, three times a day. He wasn't praying a crisis prayer, pleading for an impossible situation to be resolved. Daniel was praying a confident prayer. I was in the same situation, confident in what God was speaking into my heart. Therefore, I knew to continue praying and being faithful to Him.

Rev. Martin reminded me that when God gives a divine purpose, He also gives divine protection. I needed that reminder because He was asking me to move 1,200 miles away and step into the unknown. He ended his sermon with these words, "Move. Do it right now." No matter which sermon I listened to, God was saying these same words to me.

These sermons overwhelmed me with the same truth and the same words. I couldn't do anything except praise, weep, and worship God. I was consumed with His goodness. He knows my heart and I heard His voice loud and clear.

The next step was to get moving and follow His lead. Arizona, look out!

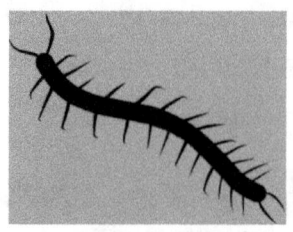

A Thousand Ways to Die in Arizona
Way #158: Centipedes

Whether it is the Banded Desert Centipede or the Giant Desert Centipede makes no difference. The latter is simply the larger relative of the former! Both species sting when they feel the need to defend themselves. The sting is quite painful and, while deaths from the stings are rare, they do happen. The venom can cause heart problems and tissue damage. Note: When walking outdoors at night, use a very bright flashlight!

Creating a road map on a vision board is one way to ensure you stay on track. Keeping a journal of events and answered prayers is another way. Staying in the Word of God is the very best way to shed light on our path. Seek Him and He will order your steps (Psalm 37:23).

REFLECTION

1. Leviticus 11:42 *"you are not to eat any creature that moves along the ground, whether it moves on its belly or walks on all fours or on many feet; it is unclean."* (HCSB uses the word 'detestable' and KJV uses "an abomination.") Abominable means "causing moral revulsion." We aren't bound to this Old Testament law any longer, but there are things that the Lord detests. Proverbs 11:20: He hates those who love to do evil. Proverbs 12:22: He hates lying lips. Luke 16:15: What is highly admired by people is revolting in God's sight. How can you be ensured you are righteous before God?

2. Confessing is agreeing with God that something is a sin. To confess is to name our sins, one by one. He already knows them but speaking them out loud to Him is a way to acknowledge them before Him. Do you need to confess your sins to God so your communication with Him is not blocked?

3. Repenting is simply deciding to turn away from sin. It is going the other way. Imagine walking down a sidewalk and then abruptly turning about face and walking in the other direction. That is a picture of repenting. Turning away from what you have been doing and going a different direction. Some sins may try to lure you back, no matter how many times you confess and repent. God's mercies are

new every morning and He knows your heart. Is there something you are struggling with or willfully keep doing?

4. Submitting is allowing God to be the boss of your life. You give up control and let Jesus take the wheel! Will you step forward today and move toward Him, following the Godward direction?

5. God *is* a Creator! He created everything in the world…everything from a bumble bee to the flower it pollinates, and the honey made from it. Close your eyes for a moment and think about all the things God created. What do you see? Journal a prayer, sharing your insights with Him.

6. Isn't it awesome to meditate on and recognize Him for all He has created? Even you and me. I hope you are listening, praying, and reading the Word.

PHOTO GALLERY

Me with my sister. I'm the barefoot one.

Me with my little brother

Mom with Eric, my oldest son, in 1983

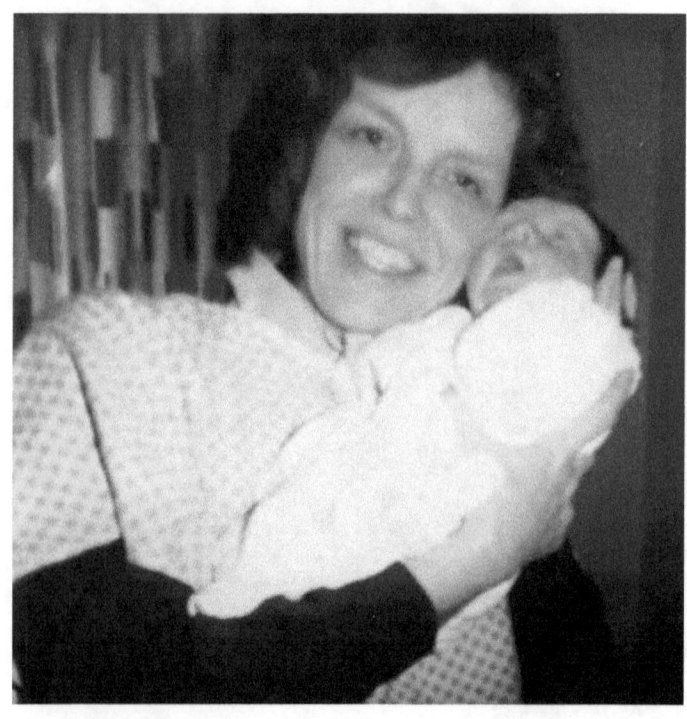

Mom with my second child, Lance, in 1985

Back 2 Skool Bash 2009 Poster

With my best friend, Racquel. We learned to pray big prayers.

The "MOVE" banner in church

The "Move" postcards on the seats

My College Graduation in 2021

Celebrating Graduation with my kids from Kansas
(Not pictured: my son in Hawai'i)

Ellie, my oldest granddaughter, at 8 years old said,
"Grammy, you have to go! You can't be like Jonah!"

With my friend, Robin, who suggested I go to The Potter's House in Dallas

Women's Prayer Breakfast, 2020, wearing my red jumpsuit

Standing on the 4th stair at The Potter's House in Dallas, Tx

Marshall, James, and me at Potter's House in Dallas. They gave me $400.

My second trip to The Potter's House with James and Pastor Dobbins

Driving to Arizona from Kansas

Volunteer Day at OCJ Kids

Pilgrim Rest Baptist Church building

*With Rev. Dr. Terry E. Mackey, Jr. at the 100 year
church anniversary celebration in 2022.*

Hiking Camelback Mountain

Meeting with Julie to discuss ministry in Phoenix

Anointed and commissioned to share the gospel

Training at OCJ Kids in Phoenix

Volunteering with Feed My Starving Children,
Pointing to my upcoming mission trip

Figure 25 Packing boxes to help a former foster youth
move into an independent living situation

With my Grandchildren

CHAPTER

10

Another Arizona Visit

My original plan was to visit OCJ Kids in Arizona on January 7 which, incidentally, was the date they were scheduled to reopen after the holidays! Since my sister and her husband were going to Arizona that week to see their grandchildren, I decided to join them. It was a 21-hour drive from Kansas, and my friend Racquel had Covid that week, so I couldn't stop half-way and stay with her. With no money for a hotel, I decided to drive straight through, which wasn't a wise decision.

It was suggested that I hug the left rear side of a semi-truck to avoid hitting large wildlife crossing the highway. Elk, horses, bears would all be hit by the 18-wheeler. I took this advice, which gave me a certain level of comfort. Driving cross country alone in the dark through the desert mountains made me nervous. Around the 19th hour driving down a mountain bend with a 6% decline, I think I may have bumped the big guy driving beside me. I don't remember clearly because I may have dozed off. I heard a loud pop and jolted awake; this I recall. Once at my sister's house, I discovered I had a broken passenger side taillight. I won't do a 21-hour solo drive again; there certainly are recorded deaths from people falling asleep at the wheel! I was blessed to come away with only a broken taillight.

The next day was a great time to relax in the nicely decorated rental home and visit casually with my sister and her daughter. Later that evening, as my niece and I were headed out to pick up dinner, I shared with her the ways God was leading me. She pulled the red Honda to the curb and parked the car. With sincerity, she turned to me and said, "Aunt Jennifer, I am just so proud of you."

A little embarrassed at the compliment, I responded, "You would do the same thing because when it's crystal clear, the only option is to obey." She said God doesn't talk to her like that, and I asked if she was talking to Him. She said she listened to a preacher by the name of T.D. Jakes; I hadn't heard of him, but I made a mental note to look him up. Arriving back at the rental house with the aroma of chicken enchiladas wafting from our delivery, we began chatting again. My niece asked my brother-in-law a question. "You listen to a lot of podcasts. Who do you listen to?"

Thinking carefully, he answered, "Well, mostly T.D. Jakes I guess." This excited me. The name T.D. Jakes had come up twice in thirty minutes. Running to the bedroom, I grabbed my cell phone, plopped down on the neatly made bed, and dialed Racquel. I couldn't remember the man's name and kept calling him Jake.[27] After sharing with her what had transpired, she confirmed the name was T.D. Jakes and that he was a biblically sound pastor who was well known. I had no idea!

The next morning, I made an appointment to visit OCJ Kids on Friday of that week. I thought God was calling me to be part of this ministry, so I wanted to check it out. When I arrived for the appointment, I met the staff and learned a little about each person, but I still did not feel a connection with the ministry or the staff. It was more of an awkwardness, which left me feeling disappointed and disconnected. It was like pulling a Gila monster off my skin. It tore at me and left me feeling pained and confused, unable to understand what God was doing.

Leaving their building, I was sad because I couldn't figure out why I wasn't a natural fit with this ministry. I slipped into my vehicle and fired up the ignition. Suddenly a smile spread across my face. "You know what I really want to do?" I thought. "I want to visit my church!"

Speaking into my phone I said, "Find directions to Pilgrim Rest Baptist Church." The GPS took me to an address that was in a part of town that did not look safe, and I didn't see a church building. I gave my phone another chance to direct me, "Call Pilgrim Rest Baptist Church." Deborah answered the phone and helped me navigate to the church. She explained there are streets and there are avenues, and I was on the wrong side of Central Avenue! This would help explain why people were meandering into traffic without a care in the world. She seemed a bit concerned for me and stayed on the line until I got to the streets side of Central Avenue. Like a child, I raised my clenched fists and squealed with excitement as I maneuvered my car into the large asphalt parking lot of the church. It felt like home! After all the years of longing for a church home, I was at MY church, and I was thrilled!

The parking lot was huge and had several rows of covered parking. Being from the Midwest, this was something new, but I was glad to be able to park in the shade near the buildings. I hurried out of the car and nearly skipped up to the church, pulling on the doors only to find them locked. I walked toward the buildings next door which included a Word Center, a café, a schoolyard, a prayer garden, and another large building that housed a gymnasium and a fitness center. I pulled on every door until I found one that opened and there sat Deborah, professional and kind, behind a plexiglass window and wearing a mask to further guard against Covid-19. Smiling from ear to ear and nearly bursting with giddiness, I asked, "Is there someone here I can talk with?"

"We usually require an appointment. Who would you like to see?" She responded nicely. Unable to contain my excitement I blurted out, "I don't care! Anybody!" Deborah picked up the receiver of a landline and turned, kind of like they do in the movies when they are saying something like, "There is a crazy lady down here and I need some help"! She hung up the phone and said someone would be down in a few minutes, and I was welcome to have a seat.

Within a few minutes, a woman approached as I paced the floor unable to sit down. She introduced herself as Elder Penn. She was exceedingly warm, friendly, and kind, with a gentle tone. She led me into an office behind the receptionist and offered me a seat. On the credenza next to the seating area was a display stand that held a single book, *"When Women Pray"* by T.D. Jakes.[28] I gasped when I saw it, clearly being led to T.D. Jakes for a purpose. I told her I needed a copy of the book, and she told me they have a bookstore, and I could buy it! And I did.

Once I was able to draw my attention back to the Elder, I shared with her a condensed version of my story. Likewise, she shared her story with me, which was like mine. She also gave me sage advice about getting involved in ministry. She said, "For six months, just come to church." She explained that God might have a different path than what I imagined, and I shouldn't jump into the thing I had always done, which was prayer, missions, hospitality, etc. She encouraged me to wait on Him and see what He was doing, saying God had her doing something she never would have imagined. She said, "Just wait on the Lord. Don't jump in too quickly. Wait on Him."

The following Sunday, 48 hours later, I arrived at the church and felt like everyone there was my new best friend. They were friendly and welcoming. As I got to my seat, I learned that Dr. Mackey and his son, Timothy, were in quarantine with COVID-19, so they would not be leading the service. I was only disappointed for a moment because then he announced that Elder Penn would be giving the message. It turned out to be a message which was exactly what I needed. The Holy Spirit was moving. Her message was real, applicable, personal, and powerful. I was blessed when I realized PRBC doesn't end their service until the work of the Holy Spirit is complete, so we lingered in worship and gave Him the time and space and opportunity to move in the hearts of those who were

> Saying it out loud made it real. But it also made it clear. I had a call. I needed to obey and find out what God had in store for me.

seeking Him. The church service lasted for over two hours, and it seemed like just a few minutes.

One day during my eleven-day stay at my sister's rental, she asked, "So, are you moving to Arizona?" I was speechless and overwhelmed. Was I? Before answering, I told her I was going to take a walk. It was a beautiful 80-degree January day with blue skies and sunshine, and I was listening to Christian radio with my earbuds. I asked, "God, is this really what you want me to do? If it is, can you let me know?" And, just as I finished praying, a new song began to play. Well, it was new to me.

The Commission, written and performed by a band called Cain, is my anthem.[29] Each time I needed an answer about something big in my life, I heard this song by Cain. All the lyrics are good, but these four lines really solidified my decision that this was God's plan.

> *Go tell the world about me*
> *You've got a purpose*
> *And I've got a plan…*
> *But goodbye is not the end.*[30]

Silent streams of tears rolled down my face as I slowly made my way back. I thanked God for such a wonderful gift of confirmation, and I went inside, looked at my sister and said, "I am moving to Arizona." Saying it out loud made it real. But it also made it clear. I had a call. I needed to obey and find out what God had in store for me.

A Thousand Ways to Die in Arizona
Way #679: The Gila Monster

It's true. There has not been a recorded death from the bite of a Gila monster in 92 years. But because of that, researchers also aren't ready to create an antivenom for a product with such low necessity.

Most people documented to have died from a Gila monster bite didn't treat the bite correctly. Apparently, pulling the monster off the skin is not a great idea because that increases the risk of severe gashes and tears, which cause more bleeding.

I'm told the bite causes unbearable pain, swelling, and a rapid drop in blood pressure. Feeling like volcanic lava surging through your veins, it is viewed as the most painful poison of any craniate. Thankfully they spend 90% of their life underground! Typically, they only surface in the warm weather.

Hikes should only happen in winter. You don't have to tell me twice. I am convinced.

The Gila monster lives underground most of the year. Indeed, this creature, much like sin, only surfaces under the right conditions. Also, like sin, it is camouflaged naturally to its environment and so may be right in front of you and remain unrecognizable. Yet, if you get too close, it will bite you with a death-enabling wound.

REFLECTION

1. Satan loves to camouflage the Truth. Proverbs 4:23 *"Above all, be careful what you think because your thoughts control your life."* Other Bible versions interpret this verse as "Guard your heart above all else, for it is the source of life." How does comparing the two explanations bring clarity to the meaning of the verse?

2. The Gila monster lives underground most of the year, patiently waiting for the right set of circumstances to find its way above ground. The sage advice from the Elder was to wait on the Lord to give an assignment. Do you find it difficult to wait on Him? Sometimes in the wait, He is allowing us a season of rest. Sometimes He is preparing us for the next season. How can you improve how you wait?

3. James 1:14-15 *"But each person is tempted when he is drawn away and enticed by his own evil desires. Then, after desire has conceived, it gives birth to sin, and when sin is fully grown, it gives birth to death."* This verse should help you recognize that the devil didn't make you do it! We are each drawn away by our own thought life. Can you think of a time when you allowed your thoughts to lead to sin? How important do you think it is to take every thought captive for Christ?

4. 2 Corinthians 10:4b,5 *"We demolish arguments and every high-minded thing that is raised up against the knowledge of God, taking every thought captive to obey Christ."* Gaining control over what you think about is a serious matter. What is a practical way you can take your thoughts captive?

5. Stop and pray. Write out a prayer to God and ask Him to show you what He has called you to do next.

6. When has God given you the wonderful gift of confirmation? Journal the details in the space below.

CHAPTER

11

God's Confirming Words

I wanted to stay in Arizona another week so I could return to church, but it was a two-day drive back to Kansas and I needed to get to work. As I drove 1,200 miles, I told the Lord how frightened I was and asked "How am I going to move to Arizona? I have no family there and I can barely pay my mortgage; now I'll have to pay rent plus the mortgage, and Arizona is twice as expensive as Kansas. How in the world can I manage that?

As I poured my heart out to Him, a phone call came in. My sister I had been staying with at the rental called to say, "We just bought a house in Arizona! We saw an open house in the neighborhood we were staying in, so we walked through, loved it, and bought it! By the way, we close at the end of February and will be in Kansas for three months, so go ahead and use the new house in Arizona until we can get there." I wiped the tears from my face, apologizing to God for doubting He had a plan. My perceived danger was nothing compared to the God I serve who, like the killer bees, is just out of sight in secret places, everywhere we can imagine.

> My perceived danger was nothing compared to the God I serve who, like the killer bees, is just out of sight in the secret places, everywhere we can imagine.

I listened to a sermon by T.D. Jakes recorded on January 16, 2022, from Acts 3:1-10 titled *The Unexpected*. He said, and I'm paraphrasing, "God is going to do the unexpected. It won't be normal. It won't be routine. It will be more than you could ask or imagine or even think. He's getting ready to blow your mind." He continued, "You're going to have such a move of God that you have to change your plans to accommodate it." Then he said, "When we go through a disruptive experience, God puts people in our path and orders our steps. I don't know who I am talking to but there is an online viewer, and I'm supposed to tell you this. This is your year to move. This is your year to take over new territory and show up in unexpected places."

His words hit home. Everything God was doing was blowing my mind, which was the expression I used when I talked to people. God was changing the plans of my entire life to accommodate His plan. Then I thought, "There are probably a million other viewers who think that word was for them, but I know it was for me." At the close of his message, T.D. Jakes reminded me that God was going to do extraordinary things, He would make it happen, and my role was to be obedient in order to break through. Then he said something *really* strange that made so much sense to me that I thought I heard him wrong. He said, "Your sister will be shattered."

One of my sisters and I are really close, both emotionally and geographically. She was already sad because, for several months, I had not been spending as much time with her in person. When I told her how God was calling me to move, she was sad that I was leaving. So, when I heard, "Your sister will be shattered," I thought, "did he seriously just say that?" It was another confirmation that God was talking to me.

Then T.D. Jakes said, "You have to move into a completely different dimension. A kingdom dimension will change your life." Hang onto that little nugget for later because we will revisit how that comes into play. He continued, "Don't go back to the familiar because that's a lie. Don't stay there. This is the Lord's doing."

Confirming Words | Francis Chan

Another sermon that spoke to me was given by Pastor Francis Chan, *Moving Forward with Excitement and Enthusiasm* from Jeremiah 1:5-8, recorded May 3, 2013. Francis Chan said, "God made your mouth…if He has empowered you, you cannot fail!" He also said, "Don't believe the lies." That statement came back over and over. A message given nine years earlier was repeating the same verses and lessons I was hearing through other pastors.

He also said when the gift is alive, it is a rush. The call on my life was a gift, it was alive, and Satan was telling me lies to make me doubt. But Pastor Chan encouraged me to obey the Lord and not be afraid. He warned that people would come against me, but I had to be obedient to God's call. He explained that Jeremiah was obedient when God called him, and it took him 30 years to have one convert. Can you imagine not giving up on God after preaching for 30 years with zero success? Talk about faith! He kept going. There was no Christian radio, no podcast, no texting a friend for prayer – it was Jeremiah and God. It was Noah and God. It was Job and God. These were real heroes who remained encouraged through their relationship with God. Brave. Faithful. Unwavering. They give us a lot to aspire to.

Confirming Words | Antoinette Staples

I listened to Antoinette Staples who said, "You are being prepared. Whatever the enemy means for evil, God means for good." She used the story of when God told Abraham to leave his family and his country (Genesis 12). She also talked about crazy faith. The story of Abraham and that term, "crazy faith" had been spoken in several sermons. This made me ponder what God was doing when so much of what I was hearing was repetitive.

She also said no matter what anybody thinks, do what God tells you to do. She mentioned the five things that happen when God speaks.[31]

1) You're going to be uncomfortable. You will hear Him talking but it won't sit well with you.

   I am a prime example! I was uncomfortable in my churches for nearly ten years. When He started speaking to me about moving to Arizona, I was hesitant. I was trying to discern if it was Him. He knew it would take a while for me to accept this as His plan, and He knew He would need to show me over and over that this was HIS voice speaking.

2) You will have natural breaks in relationships.

   I did. At church, many of the people I loved as family gradually became friendly acquaintances. I also had a breakdown of my marriage which led to a three-year separation and then divorce.

3) There will be a supernatural open or closed door.

   I thought OCJ Kids Ministries was that supernatural open door. I prayed, "I know You won't send me without a ministry so could You at least show me what that is?" Immediately, the OCJ interview was on the radio.

4) You are going to have a clear word. There's going to be a word that clearly resonates with you.

   I had the words "move" and "forward." The word "move" was in my face, all the time.

5) You will have a community to help. I had that! My friends and family were supportive. The pastor at my new church in Phoenix was supportive. My sister and her husband were buying a house in Arizona. There were many people to support and encourage me.

I marveled as I realized I hit all five indications she mentioned.

These are good markers for anyone who is trying to discern if they are hearing from God. If you don't hit all the markers, it certainly does not mean you aren't hearing from Him. We all hear from Him in different ways, usually not in an audible voice. These markers are simply a template to help us detect His voice, especially when we are just learning to recognize it.

I heard one message on loop from several pastors in the coming days. "When God calls you, you have to go. You can't revoke it." Then, Dr. Marcus Crosby at Pilgrim Rest Baptist Church was delivering a sermon and said, "Expect a blessing, look for it, and activate the plans of God. Do something with the time you've been given. God brought you here on purpose. God has plans for you."

Running through my mind was, "God has brought me here on purpose, and I need to get there." I was watching the Pilgrim Rest Baptist Church service online from Kansas, but I felt the urgency to physically get to the church. The nudge was getting stronger. I knew it was time to go.

A Thousand Ways to Die in Arizona
Way #733: Killer Bees

Africanized bees, known as killer bees, were first identified in the 1950s, and is a cross between a bee from Africa and a Brazilian honeybee. First found in the US in 1985, they are called killer bees because they have been known to chase people up to a quarter of a mile when they become defensive or excited. Such as when their hive is in perceived danger.

Over 1,000 people die from stings each year. Ninety percent of the bees in Arizona are, in fact, killer bees. They typically nest in unique places like tires, boxes, tree limbs, holes in the ground, and flowerpots.

Assume they might be everywhere and anywhere. It's looking more and more like I should stay indoors.

These bees' nest in common spaces just out of sight. They might be lurking under a mailbox or in a flowerpot or any number of places one may pass during the course of the day. Once disturbed, they relentlessly chase down the culprit and can do much damage, even to the point of death.

This reminds me of 1 Peter 5:8 that tells us to *"Be alert and of sober mind. Your enemy the devil prowls around like a roaring lion looking for someone to devour."*

One way to be alert is to be in prayer. It is an important way to start our day. Ask God to make you aware of the devil's schemes so that you are not chased down, attacked, and fooled. Another way to prepare is to wear protective clothing. The armor of God, taught about in Ephesians 6:10-18, teaches us how to protect ourselves spiritually, physically, and emotionally from the sting of Satan.

REFLECTION

1. Has your obedience to God caused others to question you or become sad at your decisions to follow Him? How did God comfort and encourage you to stay the course?

2. The prophet Jeremiah preached and prophesied for 30 years before seeing even one convert. What does this teach us about obedience and perseverance that we can imitate in our ministries?

3. Romans 8:28 reminds us that God works all things together for our good when we are walking in obedience to Him. You may feel like a swarm of bees is after you but have you seen Him turn something around to be good that you thought was destructive? Journal your answer.

4. In looking at the five markers for discerning God's voice, which one is most commonly the way you know it's Him? Review these five markers again. Is there something happening in your life right now that needs these reminders?

5. God has plans and a purpose for your life. Lean into Him and He will reveal it to you. What are your dreams, your passions, your hopes? He will meet you where you are. Jot down some thoughts and pray over them the next few days. Then, listen daily for His response.

6. Read Ephesians 6:10-17. Which of these pieces of protective armor resonate most with you today? Why?

CHAPTER

12

Open Doors

A fter returning from Arizona and listening to various online sermons all week, I went back to my home church in Kansas, New Life Community Church, where God had given me the word "move." I finally accepted the call. I voice activated it by confirming to Janet that I was moving, and God knocked my socks completely off when I saw the new sermon series: *SAY GOODBYE*. It was incredible!

The first sermon in the series was *Say Goodbye to Confusion and Hello to Clarity*. The pastor said there was something God wanted to communicate to the congregation that day. I braced myself in the chair, thinking, "OK God, I'm ready. Here I am!" I was on high alert because He was speaking to me continually. I felt there was more coming, and I had to be prepared.

The pastor talked about how confusion distracts. It does not allow focus, distorts reality, brings discouragement, and takes detours to keep us off track. The enemy doesn't want us to have clarity because he is a liar. I didn't have confusion on what I was being called to do – I was laser focused and it was great to know exactly what God said. I knew Satan would love to snatch God's call away from me. I knew I had to take every thought captive (2 Corinthians 2:5), but that was easier said than done. That's a discipline that must be developed.

In the book, *When Women Pray*,[32] written by T.D. Jakes, he gives this suggestion: Pray. Act. Keep praying. Expect miracles. Do something. After reading this, I felt God prompting me to write something He was telling me, "When you go to Arizona, you are going to have a month of being lonely, homesick, sad, and unsure." He was preparing me so I could start praying about it. Later, as those thoughts tried to haunt me, I would be able to go back to my notes as a reminder that He prepared me, and I would not believe the lies.[33]

That same day, my niece called to say she decided instead of being jealous that I could hear God's voice, she would do something about it. She said instead of worrying about things, she began to pray, count her blessings, and express her gratitude to God. She started reading His Word again and His peace filled her. She called to thank me for sharing my story with her because what God was doing in my life had impacted her. I hadn't even moved yet, and my story was changing lives. This encouraged me and I knew I needed to keep trusting His plan.

Leaving the Familiar

The Lord also spoke to me about my future saying He would lead me to a ministry that would encourage people. Earlier, He had whispered that I would start a YouTube channel. I wasn't ready then, but as the days moved forward, I knew His timing for starting that ministry was present-day. I also sensed that the YouTube channel was a place to always remember and never forget. It was no coincidence or accident that God was asking me to journal and then to share with others everything He was doing in my life! On the flip side, I didn't know how to go about setting this up, but I know where He leads, He provides.[34,35] He also revealed that I would write a book. I took note but had no intention of doing that anytime soon. But, like other things, He put His word on repeat, and I couldn't run too far from either assignment.

God was hard at work healing me from my fear of moving into the future with Him by reminding me of His track record. After all, it's not as though God and I didn't have a history. During my first marriage when my husband refused to have a Bible in the house, God provided time for me to meet with Him in secret. When I left that tumultuous relationship in terror, God provided a safe place for us to stay. When I was trying to adopt Destiny out of the foster care system, He showed up again. There were many hurdles and trials during those years, but He was faithful. In recalling His faithfulness, I was confident He would not send me to the desert alone.

I knew my time was winding down in Kansas, and I also knew I had to tell my grandkids. I took each of the five of them on one-on-one "Grammy dates." I took my eight-year-old grandchild, Ellie, to Pizza Street. We were chatting about her favorite YouTuber. With a mischievous smile I asked, "Did you know Grammy is going to be a YouTuber?" She was astounded and curious to know all about it. I told her about God calling me to start the YouTube channel, which she thought was very cool! Then, I told her God had called me to move to Arizona. She put her pizza down quickly, placed both palms on the table on either side of her plate, looked me square in the eyes, and with all seriousness she said emphatically, "Grammy, you have to go! You can't be like Jonah!" She didn't want me to leave, but even more, she didn't want me to disobey God. That was a response I didn't expect. It gave me joy to know my grandbaby understood the call and the action necessary.

After our lunch date I texted the creative arts pastor at my church, sending him a poor quality picture of a compass, asking for his expert opinion on which logo to use: the move sign with the arrow through it, like I saw on the banner during the "Move" series, or the compass, which reminds me that Jesus is my true North, the Holy Spirit is with me wherever I go, and I will go wherever He sends. He quickly responded with a cleaned up image of the compass in a .png file, letting me know this was the direction he suggested.

The Lord then told me to learn how to create the YouTube channel; I was to figure it out and there was a purpose for me to do it. I whined, "I don't want to be like Moses,[36] but You know I don't know anything about technology, so could you send somebody to help?" He responded gently but firmly, "No. I want you to learn." I did not want to learn! I did not like this answer. But He told me I was in a learning season.

Later that day I was thinking about the YouTube channel and didn't know where to begin so I started researching what was involved. I quickly learned that I needed to have four videos ready to upload before going live and would need six months of content ready with two posts per week. Overwhelmed, I was near tears. I needed 52 ideas? That could take three years to complete! (More whining ensued.) I didn't know how I would get that many ideas. As I was talking to God about how impossible it seemed to come up with ideas, I saw a Facebook post that changed everything.

> Whenever I'm overwhelmed or don't know the next step, God shows up and shows out!

In 2020 a group called View From My Window started on Facebook. Because of the pandemic, people worldwide were quarantined so they started posting a view from their window explaining where they lived and what they were looking at. Some people posted gorgeous views of rolling hills and rainbows; another posted a small crumbling cement patch that was their back patio. Nobody cared. Everyone supported and encouraged one another. The group grew to over three million people around the globe.

A woman named Susan from North Carolina posted the story of how God told Abraham to leave his family, his country, and go to a place He would show him. Here God was using the same verse with others that He used with me in telling me it was time to leave my comfortable and familiar life and follow Him. Susan wrote how God told her to move across the country from California to North Carolina. She had 1,200 comments on her post. As I read through them, there were numerous accounts of God moving many people from one place to another. He wasn't just moving me! And just like that I knew I needed to give them a way to share their story.

Without hesitation, I messaged Susan who graciously agreed to a phone call. After she shared her story, I shared mine. In my story the part that struck her was when my granddaughter told me I had to go. Susan said, "Out of the mouths of babes." I then told Susan and her husband that I wanted them to be the first guest on my YouTube channel after I moved. They were tickled that God was still using their story.

We finished our phone call, and I fell on my face and worshiped God in a puddle of tears. It would have taken me three years to develop six months of content, and He put it right in my lap. Whenever I'm overwhelmed or don't know the next step, He shows up and shows out!

A few days later I was reading *When Women Pray*. I read, "In those inevitable moments of painful uncertainty, realize that all of these women in the Bible are your sister soldiers. Draw down their strength and keep it moving."[2] I could feel the consuming power of the Holy Spirit in that moment. Thank you, Bishop Jakes!

Wildfires are prevalent in Arizona. Caused by lightning, extreme weather changes, downed power lines, or humans, whatever the reason, the dry mountain ranges make it a high-risk environment.

The fire and/or smoke can cause dangerous driving conditions. Smoke can also cause poor air quality for miles.

Stay indoors, especially if you have a heart or lung condition such as asthma. Thankfully, I do not.

I was frequently overwhelmed by the goodness of God, the magnitude of promises, and the evidence of His presence in my life. The Bible does not directly mention the term *wildfire*. However, it does talk about fire in four distinct categories: divine presence, divine judgment, refinement and transformation, and the Holy Spirit. In each instance, an all-consuming fire (wildfire) can occur, and for me, it was!

REFLECTION

1. 1 Peter 1:7 *"so that the genuineness of your faith —more valuable than gold, which perishes though refined by fire —may result in praise, glory, and honor at the revelation of Jesus Christ."* Recall a time that you had to trust God for something that seemed impossible or frightening. Do you remember what it felt like after you came through that trial? Trusting God through times like those is what builds our faith and assures us that our faith is genuine. How has your faith been strengthened by trusting Him? Write down something specific that He saw you through and spend time praising Him for it.

2. Exodus 3:2 *"The Angel of the Lord appeared to him in a blazing flame of fire from the midst of a bush; and he looked, and behold, the bush was on fire, yet it was not consumed."* When God spoke to Moses through the burning bush, he was told to remove his sandals because the ground was holy. Today, some people dress up for church services because they are meeting with Him. Whether at church or home or out in nature, wherever you go to meet and spend time with God, how do you do to honor God's presence?

3. Read Philippians 4:8. These are the things to think about when you are training your mind to take captive every thought. List them below.

4. Taking every thought captive is the secret sauce to godly living! I asked my pastor, Rev. Dr. Terry E. Mackey, Jr., "How do you stop sin in your life?" He answered without hesitation, "Moment by moment." We must take control of our thought life. James 1:15 tells us our thoughts tempt us and give birth to sin. Therefore, moment by moment we must take captive every thought and make it obedient to Christ. What thoughts do you struggle with? Be honest with yourself here. God already knows what it is.

5. I said the Lord wanted to teach me how to set up the YouTube channel. This should not sound odd to a believer. Read 1 John 2:27. How does this verse confirm that His Holy Spirit can lead us into all truth and His wisdom can reveal mysteries in how to do things, even set up technology?

6. To learn more about the fire in relation to the four distinct categories I mentioned, read Hebrews 12:29, 2 Peter 3:7, Malachi 3:2-3, and Acts 2:3-4.

13

Tell the World

I was planning to move but I didn't know why, or when, or where. I struggle with ADHD, so I tend to push too hard and get ahead of myself. It's difficult to slow down, be patient, and wait. For instance, when I decided to buy a house, the housing market was flooded with buyers and bidding wars were fierce. Each house I chose, I prayed over. Several offers were written on several different houses. Each time a competing offer won out. Then, when this particular house went on the market and it had just been newly remodeled, I jumped on it fast! I do not remember praying until afterward. I won the contract, but I don't think I was supposed to buy that house. Even as I sat and ordered blinds and rugs, I felt a tug at my heart saying not to buy things for the house. Brushing aside the nagging thoughts I pushed forward to make my house beautiful and have my own way. I did not want to make that mistake again. So, I asked Him a question, "Lord, when am I supposed to go to Arizona? You have told me to go, I am willing to go, I just don't know *when* to go. I don't want to get ahead of You."

I sensed His answer was the first of March. One night I asked Him to confirm the date because I didn't want to make a wrong move. That night I had three dreams, each different but carrying the same message. When I awoke, I knew He was telling me to go March first. Now, I could begin making real plans.

That evening, I set out to enlist people who would help with my YouTube channel. I messaged two women who commented on Susan's *View From My Window* Facebook post saying, "Hey, I have a God-story and wondered if we might chat." Both shared with me their phone numbers and I placed the calls.

The first was Cherine who lives in Queensland, Australia. She said that even though people told her she was crazy for listening to God, she knew beyond a shadow of a doubt God moved her and her husband to Australia. The next was Lin. These amazing Christian women have amazing *God Told Me to Move* stories! I also spoke with people in Florida, California, New York, and East Africa, who all said "yes" to my invitation to tell their story on my YouTube channel!

A few days later, I recall feeling oddly distant from God. I had taken my two six-year-old grandchildren on a Grammy date and then watched a KU basketball game. I hadn't drawn near to Him all day. Wanting to close the gap, I went to the Word and found Isaiah 16:22 "*When the time is right, I the Lord will make it happen.*" His Word brings me comfort. This verse was no different. I felt Him comforting my spirit and reminding me He is always with me. I was also reminded not to take a day off from spending time with Him. Time with Him is always sweet!

The next sermon in the *Say Goodbye* series from New Life Community Church was *Say Goodbye to Conformity* using the same story God impressed on my heart when He called me to move.

> "*Now the Lord said to Abram, 'Get out of your country, from your family, and from your father's house to a land that I will show you. I will make you a great nation, I will bless you and make your name great, and you shall be a blessing. I will bless those who bless you and I will curse those who curse you and in you all the families of the earth shall be blessed.' So, Abram departed as the Lord had spoken to him and Lot went with him, and Abram was 75 years old when he departed from Haran.*" Genesis 12:1-4 NKJ

God told Abraham to leave and go to the land HE *will* show him. Not a land He *has* shown him. Abraham didn't know where he was going yet he was obedient and went. My first reaction was to be thankful that God at least told me *where* to go. I still didn't know *why*.

Then the pastor said, "In order to say hello to the new things, you have to say goodbye to the old things." That was full of wisdom. I had to say goodbye to my kids, grandbabies, dog, new house, everything familiar!

Nothing in Arizona would be familiar. I would have to find the grocery stores, new doctors, everything. And the culture was different there. He also said there was no such thing as a neutral relationship. Relationships are either moving forward or backward. You are either growing in the Lord or being conformed to the world. You are either in the Word and surrounding yourself with Christian songs, teachings, and words, or you are conforming to the world. There is no middle ground. You can't be growing while deciding to take a breather. If you aren't pushing forward to grow, then you are slipping backward.

Confirming Words | Rev. Marcus McDonald

That same day, I listened to Rev. Marcus McDonald giving a message from Acts 28:1,

> *"Now when they had escaped, they then found out the name of the island was Malta. Then the natives showed us an unusual kindness and made us a fire and made us all welcome because of the rain that was falling and because it was cold. But, when Paul had gathered a bundle of sticks and laid them on the fire a serpent came out of the fire because of the heat and fastened on his hand so when the natives saw the creature hanging on his hand they said to one another, 'No doubt this man is a murderer whom, though he has escaped the sea, yet justice does not allow to live.' But he shook off the creature into the fire and suffered no harm."* NKJV

He told how a snake's teeth crisscross in such a way that when it bites someone, it's difficult to get them off, however, Paul was able to shake it off; he had a mission. God had ordered his steps, and he was going to get Paul to Rome. What I heard was that God was sending me somewhere for a reason. I was going to Arizona with a purpose.

He also said, "It is time to tell the world," which is what Paul did. Even from prison, Paul was able to share the gospel with many people. When Rev. McDonald said it was time to tell the world, I knew it was time to start the YouTube channel, which was the confirmation I needed!

Confirming Words | Dr. Terry E. Mackey, Pilgrim Rest Baptist Church

Later that day, I watched Rev. Dr. Terry E. Mackey, Jr., my pastor at Pilgrim Rest Baptist Church. His sermon was titled *From a Prayer Request To a Praise Report: How to Get a Prayer Through in 2022*, taken from Luke 17:11-19.

> *"Now it happened as He went to Jerusalem that He passed through the midst of Samaria and Galilee. Then, He entered a certain village. There He met ten men who were lepers who stood afar off, and they lifted up their voices and said, 'Jesus, Master have mercy on us!' So, when He saw them, He said to them, 'Go show yourselves to the priests' and so it was that as they went, they were cleansed. And one of them, when he saw that he was healed returned and with a loud voice glorified God and fell down at His feet giving Him thanks and he was a Samaritan. Jesus answered and said, 'Where there not ten cleansed? But where are the nine? Were there not any found who returned to give glory to God except this foreigner?' And He said to him, 'Arise and go your way, your faith has made you well.'"* NKJV

They were cleansed "as they went." They were obedient. They did what He told them to do *before* they were healed. He told them to *go* and *show* themselves to the priests, and they went. Obedience is blessed.

As they stepped, as they moved, God also moved.[38] God did not move ahead of them. He also didn't move behind them. He moved as they moved. He blessed as they were obedient. He did not bless before they were obedient, and He did not tarry with His blessing once they were obedient. He was right on time. The pastor said, "Keep moving! There's a blessing in the pressing!" Then, he again reminded me to pray BIG prayers.

> *"Now this is the confidence we have in Him, if we ask anything according to His will, He hears us."* 1 John 5:14 NKJV

Confirming Words | T.D. Jakes

In Exodus 17:1 *"At the commandment of the Lord…"* God told them to go, and they went.

In T.D. Jake's sermon entitled *Road Rage,* he discussed how travel was necessary. My ears perked up. God was requiring me to travel and now this sermon was telling me travel was necessary. I relished the way God speaks to me and thanked Him silently as I continued to listen.

This sermon was so applicable. Bishop Jakes reminded me that God will order my steps.[39] He also highlighted that God causes us to move without giving us the answers. His words were enlightening. I knew I was moving without answers, but so did Abraham and Moses and the children of Israel. Throughout the Bible people are asked to do things without the big picture laid out before them.

T.D. Jakes continued, "You must be willing to be unorthodox. Be willing to be odd and be different. Boy, was I willing to be different! People were not sure about my decision making entirely, but I knew what He told me, and Bishop was reminding me I had to be willing to do what He asked even if it seemed unconventional. He also noted that when the enemy sees destiny over our life he will attack. Consequently, we need to watch and pray and be ready. That was a good reminder to put on the armor of God every day,[40] to spend time in prayer because Satan is subtle in the way he tries to distort things. We need to have keen discernment and wisdom to handle the lies and temptations Satan will invariably throw our way. He attacks when he perceives a threat. Be careful!

Then, Bishop Jakes said that we don't want to help the snake bite us. That was the topic of the sermon I listened to earlier, which brought these two sermons together. I love how God fits the pieces together, meshing all the sermons and intertwining, overlapping, connecting, and speaking in such a powerful way. Bishop Jakes said some profound things, like:

> You can't produce what's not in you.
> You always have to be yourself.
> Just be authentic.
> Don't try to be like someone else.
> Don't try to be who you think people expect you to be.
> Just be yourself.
> Speak it how God gave it to you.[41]

_____

God has big plans for me. He isn't moving me to the middle of the desert for no good reason.

_____

He also said we are to move from place to place. "You don't know what's next. You are going to be taken away from the familiar to get to know who you are."

That struck a chord in me. I was leaving everything familiar, and I definitely didn't know what was next. He mentioned that people change in uncertainty, and when we get out of our comfort zone and allow God to stretch us, things change. Then he said, "God is getting ready to increase you," which meant there would be uncertainty, unfamiliarity, controversial issues, and I might be disliked. To increase me, God would take me outside my comfort zone, stretch me, and the stretching would hurt. Again, I was willing because He was worth it. Then he said, "Do what God calls you to do, you can't opt out of change; it's a learning season... God is putting you in a situation that is too big for you, but that doesn't mean it's not yours to do." I knew God was speaking and I journaled in big, bold marks,

GOD HAS BIG PLANS FOR ME.

**HE ISN'T MOVING ME
TO THE MIDDLE OF THE DESERT
FOR NO GOOD REASON.**

I was encouraged by Bishop Jakes to make a list of those in my circle who would pray, hold me accountable, and listen. I needed to be aware of who was in my circle and who I needed to get out of my circle; those who were not helping the process. It's never easy to let someone go but sometimes it's the right thing to do.

He also said to write the vision and make it plain by sharing it with someone and praying over it, praying in confidence. This means we have confessed our sins (which is simply agreeing with God that something is sin) and pray for God's will over the matter with assurance He will answer that prayer!

A Thousand Ways to Die in Arizona
Way #702: Flash Floods

Arizona is hot and dry, and that includes the earth. With the ground incapable of absorbing rainfall quickly, much of it runs off, which causes flash floods. Hurricanes and tropical storms over the Pacific Ocean can contribute to the amount of rainfall seen in Arizona.

Most of the year is dry, but when rain does come during monsoon season, it can fall fast and hard. One single inch of rain may cause one foot of water to flood highways and riverbanks. With the ground impenetrable, it is like pouring water on cement.

This is why school is sometimes canceled due to rain. It simply isn't safe. Keep an eye on the sky and plan accordingly. Turn around, don't drown.

Flash floods happen suddenly. Life circumstances can feel much like a flash flood at times —one thing after another takes place. It can be overwhelming and may seem like there is no way out. However, God assures us that when the storms come, He is there. He is our strong tower. He is our safety. After all, *"even the wind and the sea obey Him"* (Matthew 8:27).

REFLECTION

1. Proverbs 18:10 *"The name of Yahweh is a strong tower: the righteous run to it and are protected."* Have you had to run to get out of the rain? Maybe you ran to the alcove of a storefront or similar place to get out of a sudden downpour. This reminds me of what it's like to run to Jesus. He is strong and we are protected. What image does this verse (Proverbs 18:10) bring to your mind?

2. Psalm 46:1 *"God is our refuge and strength, an ever-present help in trouble."* We do not need to feel overwhelmed. We need to simply communicate with Him. He hears us. He is able to help us. He desires that we listen to Him. How can you best listen to Him when you are overwhelmed? (Hint: you need to start practicing your answer before you are overwhelmed next.)

3. Hebrews 13:8 *"Jesus Christ is the same yesterday and today and forever."* Does this verse bring you comfort? Why or why not?

4. Satan has a subtle way of trying to distort things. When he sees the destiny over our life, he works overtime to throw us off course. Has this happened to you? What are some of the distractions, lies, and roadblocks Satan has put in your path to confuse or distract you? How do you overcome his attempts so you can stay on course?

5. Do you daily put on the armor of God? Read Ephesians 6:10-20 and in the space below, draw a stick figure wearing these articles of clothing. What does each article represent?

6. How has God intertwined, overlapped, and connected things in your life to speak to you and get your attention? He does this through music, sermons, lyrics, and everyday things, like nature. Be on the lookout – keep your eyes and ears open to repeated things in your life – it's most likely God trying to get your attention.

CHAPTER

14

Deliberate Obedience

At this point, I had not heard back from OCJ Kids Ministry. It seemed God had spoken so clearly about being part of this ministry, yet I had not received any communication from them. I didn't understand what He was doing, but I knew God had called me to Arizona, and I knew obedience was the only way forward. I returned to my journaling and timeline to remind me of the steps God led me in pursuing Him and the move to Arizona, pushing aside the lies of the schemer and leaning into God. I needed to pray BIG prayers.

When God is silent it doesn't mean He is still. He is always moving. We just can't always see what He is doing. That's why it is important to journal what God says. Write it down, word for word, so there is no question later. The father of lies tries to twist what God says to confuse us and make us doubt. Genesis 3 tells the story of Eve and the serpent. Satan used God's words and twisted them enough to make her doubt God. *"Did God really say, 'You can't eat from any tree in the garden?'"* Satan insinuated that a good and kind God would surely not have said such a thing, and she must be mistaken. Satan caused her to doubt what she knew to be true. That is why we need to journal word for word what God speaks. Paraphrasing and shorthand notes give way for Satan to swoop in and cause confusion and doubt. Remembering this, I encouraged myself with a sermon Dr. Tony Evans preached from Mark 4:35-41,

> *"On the same day when evening had come, He said to them, 'Let us cross over to the other side.' Now when they had left the multitude, they took Him along the boat as He was. And other little boats were also with Him. And a great windstorm arose, and the waves beat into the boat, so that it was already filling. But He was in the stern asleep on a pillow. And they awoke Him and said to Him, 'Teacher, do you not care that we are perishing?' Then He arose and rebuked the wind, and said to the sea, 'Peace, be still.' And the wind ceased and there was a great calm. But He said to them, 'Why are you so fearful? How is it that you have no faith?' And they feared exceedingly and said to one another, 'Who can this be, that even the wind and the sea obey Him?"* NKJV

In going to the other side, the disciples were doing what Jesus told them to do. They were following directions, but they were afraid because of the storm. Jesus laid down and fell asleep. He was not afraid; He knew they would get to the other side, but the disciples were scared because they saw the storm. They had seen big storms on this body of water before. They may have seen boats tipped over or even known people who had drowned in one such storm. We don't know. But we do know they allowed their worries and cares to cause them to take their eyes off Jesus.

> Obedience doesn't keep us from the storms, but it will get us where God intends for us to go.

I thought about that. God didn't tell them to go halfway across and drown. He told them to go to the other side. I realized that, even in the middle of the journey, there will be storms and turbulence and things that happen that might be scary.

But during this particular storm in the Scripture, Jesus was asleep, and he didn't just nod off with the gentle rocking of the boat. No, Mark

4:38 tells us He had gotten a pillow and laid down intentionally! Jesus was not afraid. He knew they were going to get safely to the other side. Obedience doesn't keep us from the storms, but it will get us where God intends for us to go.

The Move to Arizona was Falling into Place

At this time, I had worked remotely for the same company for six years, only going into the office for monthly sales meetings. It's a small business and my boss was the owner and CEO. Since the pandemic, we had switched our monthly meetings to Zoom calls so, having accepted the call to follow God to Arizona, I needed to call my boss and ask if I could keep my job. Taking a deep breath to steady my resolve, I called him on video conference and told him about my decision, sharing how God had directed my decision every step. As I related the story, he said he had "goosebumps," and agreed that I could work remotely even from Arizona. God's faithfulness, provision and orchestration continues to overwhelm me. I could move 1,200 miles away and still have a job, an income, and financial stability.

In February 2022, He told me I needed to get my YouTube channel running by the end of the month. He knows I work best with a deadline, so He gave me one. I researched and found videos online that explained how to start my own channel. Where God sends, He provides, and He did. Because I'm not tech-savvy, it was frustrating, but I had the first five steps I needed and was able to accomplish them through tears and crying out to God. He loves me and shows me so much grace and mercy, and I try not to whine so much.

I created my first YouTube episode, which was very unprofessional because I didn't have proper lighting or sound. I spilled my heart in fifteen minute segments by simply sharing my story. Episode by episode, I shared what God was doing in my life.[42] Gradually, I began sharing sermons and Bible lessons, remembering how Elder Penn advised me not to jump into ministry too soon because the temptation would be to go into something familiar. T.D. Jakes told me not to go back to the familiar because it's a lie.[43] He warned viewers not to stay there and reminded me, "This is the Lord's doing." Many sermons by various pastors repeated the same idea. Don't believe the lies of the devil. Keep moving forward in obedience into God's bigger plan.

One Sunday morning in February, I joined my new church online, Pilgrim Rest, where Dr. Terry Mackey was sharing how, during Bible times, stories were told orally because they didn't have printers, books, and technology like we have today. Stories were orally shared from generation to generation. That is exactly what God told me to do. Tell my story. There is power in sharing what we have been through and how God came through.

Dr. Mackey said, "What God puts in place, no man can reverse." That was the same message I heard before. It reminded me that if God called me to it, it was mine to do.

Later that day, I listened to another T.D. Jakes's sermon entitled, *When Faith Crosses the Line* from Matthew 15:21-29. The scripture text talks about the woman that wanted healing for her daughter and how she crossed geographical boundaries, cultural boundaries, and theological boundaries. I could relate – I crossed geographical boundaries moving from Kansas to Arizona; cultural boundaries by going to a predominantly black church, which ushered me across theological boundaries because the black theology identifies the Christian faith in relation to political justice.

The passage says that Jesus *"answered her not a word."* She kept pressing. She crossed over His silence and went into a new region. Bishop Jakes reminded me to step out of my region and enlarge my territory. I also wrote the word "healings." I later realized I had jotted that word down just like that seven times over the course of three months. It kept coming to me in the middle of nowhere and I didn't know why. I asked the Lord, "Am I going to heal in Jesus' name?" That scared me. It was exciting but also frightening because that would mean going outside of my comfort zone even more and I would have to be willing to look like a fool. God answered, "Just be ready. Be available. Change is coming."

He reminded me it isn't what we say, it's what we do. We've all been told that actions speak louder than words, and it is true. My actions of being obedient and moving across the country spoke to so many people!

It reminded me of a former coworker who had referred to me as a tenacious bulldog. I had been told that I like to push, so I suppose that can be a good thing when used correctly.

"Obey even when it is silent," Bishop Jakes encouraged. The Israelites had 400 years of silence! I was upset when I had two days of silence. I cannot imagine 400 years of encouraging myself! But I have learned that when God is silent, it doesn't mean He isn't working. He is always working. To wrap up his sermon, he said, "There are times you have to move forward when God says nothing at all." (My words: Move. Forward.)

He also said we are to be willing to move and to take responsibility. "**'I will'** is our answer to God's **'I AM.'**" He shared how the prodigal son didn't get the ring on his fingers, the new robe, or the fatted calf until he went home, "The provision was conditional on the place; there's something about being in the right place."

Permission to Go

I was still in Kansas at this juncture, learning at the feet of Bishop T.D. Jakes. Faith is radical and yes, moving across the country is radical! Doing the absurd because God said to. Not being afraid to be unconventional. He used the example of Jesus going to Tyre and Sidon. These were controversial cities for Him. They were Gentile towns, not Jewish towns. The Jews knew the Messiah was coming. The Old Testament talked about it, and they believed it. Where they got it wrong was that they thought He would be a political leader. They didn't understand that He would be The King of the universe, King of Kings! They thought He would be the political leader of the Jews. So, when He went and spoke to the Gentiles and even the Gentiles could be saved—the Jews did not like that! It was controversial! That was radical! Bishop Jakes encouraged me that even if He calls me to something that sounds a little coo-coo, I have to trust Him. Even if I don't get results! The results are not up to me.

One thing Bishop Jakes said in this particular sermon that unnerved me was to be acquainted with grief. That does not sound pleasing! Even though I wasn't sure what was coming down the pike, I knew I needed to start praying about it because it was surely coming. He also preached that rejection was part of the deal. When we serve Christ, we will be rejected like He was. That is not an excuse to bow out.

God told me to leave Kansas on March 1, but He said I didn't have to be in Arizona until March 6. I pondered that because I couldn't figure out why I had an entire week when it only took two days to get there. Contemplating this with my friend, Robin, she suggested that maybe I was supposed to go to The Potter's House in Dallas.

I sat up straight as an arrow and inhaled a deep breath of excitement and exclaimed, "Maybe I am supposed to go to The Potter's House!" Filled with excitement, we talked about how I could stay with my friend in North Texas, and I could actually make it happen! I began to pray about it. God is this what you want? Could I go and meet T.D. Jakes? The thought had me giddy.

That evening, I sat on the sofa with my laptop. Before tuning in to a new sermon, I prayed, "Lord, do I have permission to go to The Potter's House in Dallas?" The sermon I wanted to watch was the newest one T.D. Jakes had uploaded. I found it and saw it was titled, *You Have Permission*. I smiled. Then, in the sermon, Bishop Jakes said something like, "that thing you are wanting to pursue, God is saying you have permission." It was in that instant that I clicked the pause icon on the screen and began to weep. God really hears me when I pray, and I was washed afresh with the realization that He is magnificent.

"Stand and see doesn't mean don't move.
Nothing will stop the plan of God."
Pastor Kenneth Martin, Greater Archview
Baptist Church, Little Rock, AR

"Often when God wants to do something FOR you,
He will ask something FROM you first."
Dr. Tony Evans

"Your next move is so important; you can't afford to miss the turn.
It's not a destination. It's a decision. Decide to be there!"
Michael Phillips, The Potter's House Dallas

I was fully convinced that I was not to believe the lies of the devil because God's word cannot be revoked. I was to move and transition into the place and time of God's plan.

A Thousand Ways to Die in Arizona
Way #958: Falling off a Mountain

There are people who fall into the Grand Canyon and off many of the other mountain range trails each year in Arizona. Hikers need the proper footwear unless they plan to walk a flat path, and then tennis shoes are acceptable. Get gear. Be prepared. Hike with care. Noted.

Some people intentionally fall off a mountain to their death, which is sad. Others are simply trying to get a selfie with the perfect shot and lose their balance. An average of twelve people a year die at the Grand Canyon. While most falls essentially cover someone from head to toe in contusions, abrasions, and lacerations, multiple internal injuries and broken bones can also happen. If planning a hike in Arizona, be prepared with the proper equipment, water, and first aid.

Oh, and don't take a selfie on a mountain. Be safe up there.

I mentioned that people fall to their death in the Grand Canyon each year, but people also fall on regular mountain trails. Wearing the proper footwear and using hiking poles is smart. I took a friend hiking, and she literally went out in a helicopter after falling on a steep incline of nothing except dirt. She broke her ankle in two places. It was horrifying, but she didn't die, thank God, like others have.

In 2010, I fell off a mountain. I didn't realize then that I didn't have the proper equipment. That epiphany came some years later when I was reading through my journal and noticed I had written to be careful of a wolf in sheep's clothing in my church. I had not prayed through that warning, so it snuck up on me. After all those years enjoying my mountain top experience, something so grievous occurred that I had to leave the church after 23 years.

Like hiking a mountain trail, life can be treacherous navigating the slippery slope of change, transition, and grief. We have to be prepared to listen to God, to pray fervently, and to follow Him through obedience in the direction He leads. He holds back the avalanche of emotions and the disapproving words and looks we get from those who don't understand the life of obedience. Walking with Him is the most secure place we can ever hope to be. He keeps us from falling.

REFLECTION

1. Have you ever been in a storm and wondered how God was going to get you out of it? Or maybe you wondered even *if* He would get you out of it! How does trusting Him change how you feel about the situation?

2. Journal the things you hear from the Lord. Do not just jot a note. Make it plain so there is no margin for misunderstanding or second guessing when you go back to read it. Write your thoughts, ideas, and prayers clearly so when you go back, you have a concise record of what was said, how you interpreted it, and the emotions you felt.

3. Mountains do not move. They are massive in size and rooted in the earth. They are the definitive symbolic representation of stability and security. They also have religious symbolism since one could be "closer to God". They speak of our high points in life as well as our low points. God uses the imagery of mountains and valleys to help us understand. Read Psalm 121:1-2 *"I lift my eyes towards the mountains. Where will my help come from? My help comes from the Lord, the Maker of heaven and earth."* This verse assures us that we do not journey alone. God is with us, and he never sleeps or gets tired. He watches over us, so we do not stumble and fall. Write two or three sentences to tell God how this makes you feel.

4. Read Mark 11:23. *"For assuredly, I say to you, whoever says to this mountain, 'Be removed and be cast into the sea,' and does not doubt in his heart, but believes that those things he says will be done, he will have whatever he says."* There is nothing God cannot do. He is sovereign. He is all-powerful and He alone has authority. Do you believe He is able? Why or Why not?

5. Read Luke 4:29-30. *"They got up, forced Jesus out of town, and took Him to the edge of the cliff on which the town was built. They planned to throw Him off the edge, but Jesus walked through the crowd and went on His way."* The people were opposed to the truth and would do anything to quiet Him down. Yet Jesus would not fall off the mountain, nor would He be thrown off the mountain. He is sovereign and He simply passes through them unharmed. Has anyone ever indicated they did not want to hear what you had to say? How did you handle it? How might you handle it in the future in light of this lesson?

6. Read 1 Corinthians 13:2. *"And though I have the gift of prophecy, and understand all mysteries and all knowledge, and though I have all faith, so that I could remove mountains, but have not love, I am nothing."* All spiritual gifts are for the edification of the church body. However, Paul explains that the gifts are worthless and of no use to the body of believers if they are done without love. What does this mean to you? How would you describe the love he is referring to in this verse?

CHAPTER

15

Time to Go

March 1 was coming quickly. Things went fairly quickly once I answered the call. I was learning how to create a YouTube channel while packing and saying my goodbyes, which was bittersweet, but I knew beyond a shadow of a doubt it was the right decision. I went through my clothes to determine what to pack. Most of my clothes are dated hand-me-downs from my sisters and were not difficult to part with, and moving to Arizona, I assumed I would only need summer clothes, or so I thought. I packed a tub of things I could get by with and bagged up more to donate to a local thrift store. In looking through the closet, I came across Destiny's red pant suit that she didn't intend to wear again, so I asked for her permission to take it with me to Arizona. I didn't know why I felt compelled by the Lord to take it, but she said I could have it, and I hung it on the grab handle in the backseat of my car, which was already packed with six tubs. Two were filled with work supplies, two contained kitchen and household items, and two held clothes and shoes.

As I drove away from my newly purchased home in the predawn hours of the morning on March 1, 2022, I thought I would cry, but tears didn't come. That sinking feeling of loss and aloneness I thought I would have simply didn't consume me. I was sad, but I was also excited to see what

God had in mind. I drove all day down the stark, straight highway that is Interstate 35 to get to my friend's house in North Texas, which sits in a quiet neighborhood of homes on about one acre of land each, giving it a bit of a country feel. After pulling carefully into her switchback driveway, I got out of the car to stretch my back and legs. Heading slowly into the house, I was greeted with the smell of a freshly baked brisket and my friend's welcoming hug that enveloped me.

The following evening, we set out to The Potter's House. Sunday, I heard Bishop Jakes announce that the doors open one hour before church, and I was sure it would be a packed house. That meant leaving during rush hour traffic…in Dallas…but my friend was a trouper! She drove her SUV expertly through the ten lanes of traffic seemingly unaffected by the many vehicles constantly merging on or exiting off the freeways.

The weather was great, and the sky was clear. As we neared our destination, she pointed out the church from a distance and I quickly took several pictures with my smartphone. It was incredibly exciting to be attending The Potter's House service, and I was very hopeful that T.D. Jakes would be in the house!

As we slowed to pull off the highway toward West Kiest Boulevard, we were surprised to see many orange construction barrels and several police cars with their blue and red lights flashing up ahead. We thought perhaps there had been a car wreck or some other catastrophic event, but as we meandered our way through the makeshift detour and pulled up closer to the entrance of the expansive church parking lot, we realized it was simply security. Whether in anticipation of a large crowd or because Bishop Jakes has celebrity status, or both, I don't know.

My friend lowered the window as we approached, and a uniformed officer asked if we were here for The Potter's House. Seeing us nod, he motioned for us to enter the property.

Imagine my surprise when there were only a few cars there! We drove around the massive parking area trying to determine which door was the entrance. Finally, we noticed someone walking toward the church and we were able to inquire. Ultimately, we parked in a spot near a light post so it would be easy to locate when we came out.

I slipped easily out of the black leather captain's chair in my friend's red SUV and sprang into the parking lot giddy with excitement. I took in the front wall of the building. Situated just beyond an expansive cement forecourt, it welcomed us with an extensive glass façade under a portico held up by seven pillars. I marveled that even the construction of the building tells God's story. Under the portico, there were ten sets of double doors. Above it, the name of the church was announced in large lettering, The Potter's House. I couldn't believe I am there! As we walked near the entrance, a gentleman opened the door for us, or so we thought. He told us the doors do not open until 6:30. We had a thirty-minute wait. Feeling disappointed, we walked back to the car to wait. Finally, when the time arrived, we made our way back to the same door. This time when the gentleman opened it, he welcomed us in!

The entryway foyer was grand! A wide-open space sprawled to the left and the right with so much to explore but my gaze fixed on the doors leading into the sanctuary. I beelined for the door. My friend asked where I wanted to sit and I quickly replied over my shoulder, "The stage!" One of the ushers must have overheard me because she followed me down the carpeted aisle past rows and rows of wooden pews covered in durable, crimson-colored fabric. As I neared the front of the church she said, "Ma'am, ma'am" trying to get my attention. "You can't go up there ma'am!" I was already smiling with excitement as I turned to her and replied, "I am not really going to sit on the stage. I just want a picture." As I began to ascend the seven steps that lead to the stage (again with seven, the architect knew a thing or two about the Bible) she insisted I could not go on the stage. I stopped on the fourth stair and turned towards the spacious auditorium filled with 8,200 seats. I spread my arms out wide, and my sister snapped the picture before the usher could protest, and then I was off the steps and introduced myself to her. Her name was Maxine, and she came over and took a picture with me before telling me, not so sternly, to stay seated.

The nearly empty but enormous sanctuary gulped us up as we found our way to a seat front and center of the stage. Two young men were sitting at the end of the pew by the center aisle. One of them introduced himself as James and asked where we were from. I told him that I am from Kansas City, visiting my friend who lives in North Texas. He then asked what brought me here from Kansas. That is all the invitation I needed! I got up and crossed in front of my friend to sit beside James and tell him all the God things that had transpired and all that He had told me to do. I told him about YouTube and my move and the reason I was there that night. He also shared that he had just started a YouTube channel, and he understood the trials I had gone through figuring out how to accomplish that. (Find him @kingjames1934.)

As we visited, he motioned toward his seatmate Marshall, and I later discovered they had sent me $400 on Cash App! I did not ask them for money or to my knowledge even indicate I needed it. What I did know was that I left Kansas with enough gas money to get to Dallas. I was not yet sure how I would get to Arizona. I only trusted that God had a plan.

Geopolitical outcomes such as Russia's invasion of Ukraine in late February of 2022 likely had a big impact on gas prices, but whatever the reason, they were on the rise and fast. The national average hit $4 a gallon the first week of March that year. That was a shock to me, needing to travel by car 1,200 miles with a miniscule budget. Nevertheless, this was no surprise to God and just look at Him provide!

As we spoke, the music began, and we rose to our feet to worship our Lord and Savior. The music touched my soul as they sang but when the first words out of Pastor Venshard Dobbins mouth were, "Genesis chapter number one" I knew. I just knew. God was starting at the very beginning because this, THIS, was only the beginning. I listened intently as the pastor continued. His sermon title was *Use Your Voice*. He spoke about moving and speaking and using whatever platform God gave you. He cited YouTube as his example.

James and I kept glancing at one another in disbelief. Everything he was saying from the pulpit was everything we had just discussed prior to the service! It was like he was cementing what God had told each of us to do, filling in every crack and crevice to shore up any unsettling. It was unnerving and exciting at the same time. At one point James made a motion with his hands to represent his mind was blown and I had to agree. We both shed tears in awe of our God. "God told me to tell you to move, but it's not enough for you to move if you're not going to move and speak." His words kept ripping away at my doubts.

Before the service began, I had put my friend on notice that I wanted to stay after it concluded in hopes of speaking to the pastor. I wasn't aware at the time that Bishop Jakes would not be present. That was of little concern to me afterward because God had been there and that was what mattered. I stood with my hands resting on the back of the pew in front of me at the conclusion of the service and I bowed my head, closed my eyes, and talked to God. I told Him that if I was really doing this thing —if I was really leaving Dallas and moving to Arizona, I would like Him to confirm it again. This time, I wanted the pastor to come over and pray with me.

I wanted to share my story with him in hopes of receiving wise counsel and someone to tell me I was not crazy. What he gave me was worth so much more. The pastor was a tall man, slightly over six feet. He was standing on the second or third step between the floor and the stage and six or seven people gathered around him to chat. I stopped praying, opened my eyes and looked at him and he looked directly at me. He walked toward me, put his hand on my hand, and began to pray for me! Next, he put his other hand on my head and prayed an anointing prayer over me. Then, he said something I won't forget, "And that book God told you to write…He's telling me to tell you to write it." I shared a brief snippet of my story with him, and he simply said, "Obey."

When I left my friend's house the next morning, I drove to Albuquerque on cloud nine. More convinced that my calling was real. I planned to spend a couple of days at Racquel's before driving the final leg of the trip to Phoenix. My devotion for Lent while I was there said, "Jesus's personal authority is such that He simply gives the order to 'follow Me' and they leave behind family, possessions, and security, even though they don't know where they are going. There is no argument, no delay, no excuse, only immediate compliance with Jesus's words. Jesus still expects the same from us today. The urgency of His mission requires an immediate response. His authority is so great that when we hear His call there is no option but to follow Him, trust His provision, and joyfully serve-at once."[44]

Again, God confirmed in my spirit that I was doing what He called me to do, and I was continually amazed at how God was working and constantly reassuring me. I was also aware that my physical move caused a spiritual move in the hearts of numerous others. Your actions also speak, so be careful!

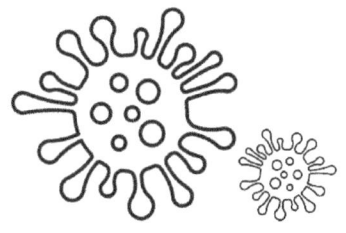

A Thousand Ways to Die in Arizona
Way #999: Valley Fever

Apparently, there is a fungus that lives in the soil in the southwestern United States and, when inhaled, it can cause a deadly infection. People aged 60 and older are most susceptible.

Indeed, I am 60. Keep an N65 mask in the glove box of the car. 10-4.

God stirs the wind and things happen! The wind carried the plague of darkness in Exodus and the wind carried the heat that scorched the head of Jonah. It blew across the wilderness and struck the four corners of the house that fell on Job's children. It held back the Red Sea so the children of Israel could pass by.

God stirs the wind in our lives, too, and brings about change. We only need to be cognizant of the sound of His voice so that we are not rattled by the wind, but instead, we are comforted.

REFLECTION

1. Read Exodus 10:13. *"Then the Lord said to Moses, 'Stretch out your hand toward the sky so that darkness spreads over Egypt – darkness that can be felt."* As a child, I remember being scared of the dark. Now, as an adult, I know that darkness hides from light, and He is the light of the world. In Him, there is no darkness (1 John 1:5). Have you ever felt the darkness? How is it different from the light?

2. Read Exodus 14:21. *"Then Moses stretched out his hand over the sea, and all that night the Lord drove the sea back with a strong east wind and turned it into dry land."* God sent an angel ahead of the Israelites and behind them to protect them. When they felt trapped, God brought about deliverance. Have you seen God's protection and provision in your life? Explain.

3. Read Job 1:19. *"When suddenly, a mighty wind swept in from the desert and struck the four corners of the house. It collapsed on them, and they are dead, and I am the only one who has escaped to tell you!"* Have you heard the phrase, "God is the God of suddenly" Have you ever experienced Him moving in your life in a sudden and unexpected way?

4. If you have experienced Him as "God of the suddenly," how did you respond?

5. Read Jonah 4:8. *"When the sun rose, God provided a scorching east wind, and the sun blazed on Jonah's head so that he grew faint. He wanted to die, and said, 'It would be better for me to die than to live."* Did you notice when Moses stretched out his hand in Exodus, God sent an east wind? Likewise in this verse, the wind came from the east. Why did God send the wind from the east? What significance does it have? (If you aren't sure, that's ok. As you continue to read, you will discover the answer.)

6. When was the last time you were amazed by God? Explain.

16

Let Down Your Nets

As I crossed the state line from New Mexico to Arizona on March 5, 2022, it began to rain. I had a strong sense that God was washing me clean and giving me a new beginning. When I glanced out the passenger window, I witnessed the most magnificent rainbow! Tears stung my eyes as I marveled at the way God speaks. I had no idea how often it rained in the desert, but it seemed like a miracle to me, so unexpected and affirming. Later I learned that there are an average of only four days in March when rain can be expected in Arizona. Indeed, it was a rare occurrence! Incidentally, snow has only been recorded four times in March since 1896. This brings me to a point: the number four had come up several times throughout my 1,200 mile trip.

I also noticed from my picture taken inside The Potter's House that I was standing on the 4th step of the stage and my cash app had $400 arrive. On the fourth day of creation, God created the sun, moon, and stars to rule the day and night and to divide the four seasons.

According to Strong's Concordance, the original Hebrew word used in Genesis 1:14 is *"moed,"* which translated means *appointed time or divine appointment.* Additionally, Hebrews 2:4 states the four witnesses of God on earth are signs, wonders, miracles, and gifts of the Holy Spirit. If that wasn't enough, the rainbow is referenced in exactly four chapters of the

Bible (Genesis 9, Ezekiel 1, Revelation 4, Revelation 10). Suffice it to say that the number four was in my face, and I was paying attention.

After witnessing the rainbow and feeling like all the dust from driving through the New Mexico desert had been washed off my car, the rain stopped as suddenly as it began. I knew God was confirming my move to Arizona.

I pulled my freshly rinsed sedan into my niece's driveway in Florence, Arizona in the late afternoon and sighed with a smile. I had arrived; I was home. I was going to stay a couple of nights with her until my furniture arrived on March 7, 2022. Arizona has master planned communities that are basically micro towns dropped here and there in the desert, surrounded by nothing. The micro town has a small grocer's, a gas station, a bank, a McDonald's, a health clinic, a church, a school, a community center, and about 5,000 homes. It's beautifully landscaped and has lots of amenities, but there is no actual town for miles, which is so odd to this Kansas native.

The next morning, I attended Pilgrim Rest Baptist Church with anticipation of joining their membership role that morning. The Sunday morning sermon was about God taking our darkest moment and turning it into our shining moment. He said some doors are not open so we can get out, but so others can get in. I had been on a Zoom call with the pastor a few weeks earlier to tell him I was coming to Arizona and planning on joining his church. When I walked to the front of the church after the service, he didn't recognize me because I was wearing a mask due to Covid protocols. So, I smiled big and raised my eyebrows and my shoulders in a silent "eeeeek" of excitement and suddenly, the realization of who I was registered in his eyes. He welcomed me with an outstretched hand and introduced me to the congregation, sharing how God had moved me 1,200 miles to be part of their family. After the service, several people gave me fist bumps and waves and introduced themselves. This was my new church, and it felt like home. It was awesome. This was my shining moment.

Just as God had prepared me, moving to a new place and starting over would take effort and not be easy. And true to His word, that March was difficult. Remember, God said, *"When you go to Arizona, you are going to have a month of being lonely, homesick, sad, and unsure."* I knew it would be hard, but I thought I was ready. I had prayed and thought I had come to terms with the relocation.

I moved into my sister's house the following Monday when the furniture was delivered. I didn't have cell service or internet, and I was absolutely alone. No television, no smartphone, no music. Silence. My own thoughts, fears, and anxieties raced through my head. I went to my niece's house during the day to work and then went back to my house.

With nowhere else to go, the highlight of my day was cruising down to McDonald's to get out of the house for a bit. The sky was blue, the ground was brown. I felt like I would never see a cloud or a rainbow again. The newness of the perfectly clear blue sky and 70-something degree weather had worn off and I needed some diversity. It was strange what I missed when I no longer had it, so I decided to set my mind on things above and not let my situation dictate my attitude. Rejoice in the Lord always, right? Feelings are not facts.

In the evening, I would drive to the community park and walk the paved path around the small but gorgeously manicured lake, talking with God for an hour or two before heading home. I didn't know about the javelina yet, or I wouldn't have been so brave.

God reminded me to be deliberate and stay in His will. Being deliberate is key. I wasn't going to stay in the will of God by accident. I had to open my Bible; I had to study my Bible. I spent time in prayer, always learning and seeking and striving to grow spiritually. I didn't want to go backwards by sitting still spiritually. There was to be no pause. God had my undivided attention. Dr. Evans said there was going to be an opportunity to see God at an entirely new level. That "Kingdom Dimension" Bishop Jakes referred to came quickly to my mind as he urged me not to fear the circumstances. God is up to something worldwide and I was to believe God for the victory.[45]

One day I heard my cell phone ding, which surprised me because I still didn't have service. When I checked, I had a notification that T.D. Jakes had uploaded a new sermon to YouTube. I clicked on the notification banner and was able to listen to the two-hour broadcast before the signal dropped. God was making sure I only heard the voices He wanted me to hear during this time. After ten days of this, I needed encouragement and God sent that to me through my YouTube channel audience, which I was able to receive when I was working at my niece's house during the day.

I started receiving messages from viewers thanking me for telling my story and for encouraging them to get into the Word. They were getting back on the right track, dusting off their Bibles. They were praying again and journaling their prayers. They thought I was helping them, but I knew they were actually helping me. Some people called, some emailed me, others texted or reached out on social media. It was a great week to hear from so many people that God was on the move. People were using their proverbial flashlights, and they were watching their step.

Nevertheless, just a few days later I was homesick. Not for Kansas, but I wanted my kids and grandkids to come to Arizona. I felt like the disciples on the boat in the middle of the storm. I knew God told me to "go" and that He would get me safely to the other side. I knew He can be trusted, but I was in the storm and needed to hold on to victory. He wouldn't get me halfway there and leave me. He would get me safely to the other side. Encouraging myself in the Lord became a habit I had to hone regularly.

The third Sunday at my new church, they were selling tickets to a Women's Prayer Breakfast. I didn't know what that was, but I bought a ticket. Then I learned the theme was to wear red. Immediately I remembered Destiny's red pantsuit I had packed. Incredible how God thinks of everything and made sure I had what I needed. When I got home, I tried it on, and it fit perfectly.

Another miracle happened that same Sunday. I rarely had wireless service at home, so when I heard my phone ding, I jumped up because I couldn't believe a notification had come through. Typically, if this happens I have anywhere from a split second to a couple of minutes of service. I decided to try to listen to the second service at my home church, Pilgrim Rest. There was a guest preacher that day and he was not only a friend of the Rev. Dr. Terry E. Mackey, Jr. He was also a friend of Pastor Kenneth Martin. I was anxious to listen to Dr. George Parks of Little Rock, Arkansas's New Hope Church.

He preached on Psalm 134 a sermon titled *All Night Long*. He said, "God sees what you need" and "He never started a job He didn't finish." I knew God wouldn't leave me in the storm, and this helped solidify that confidence. Additionally, I was able to listen to another sermon, so I went to The Potter's House and listened to Bishop Eric McDaniel preach a sermon titled, *Exhausted, but Still in Pursuit*. He reminded me to "Go on the strength that you have and go do what God called you to do!"

I find it overwhelming to hear from God in such direct ways. When He speaks to exactly the issue I am facing, it just blows me away.

There are a plethora of sermons on YouTube and a multitude by Dr. Evans! Each time I prayed before opening my computer, and each time God gave me the exact words of encouragement and increased knowledge I needed. Piece by piece, things were coming together.

> The blessings of obedience follow me.

> *"I am Yahweh, your Holy One, Creator of Israel, your King, look! I am about to do something new! Even now it is coming, do you not see it? Indeed, I will make a way in the wilderness, rivers in the desert."* Isaiah 43:15

I was and am overwhelmed by His presence and the way He speaks to me. It is not lost on me that I am in the middle of the wilderness. I am in the desert. But I know God has sent me here for a reason. In His timing, it will unfold, and it will be wonderful and more than I can hope for or imagine, because the blessings of obedience follow me.

On Good Friday, I went to a community called Cooper Basin for a pedicure. A young mother sitting next to me started to chat, so I shared my story with her, excitedly telling her how God made it clear I was to move to

Arizona to share the gospel. She invited me to her church for their Good Friday service. I was overjoyed and agreed to meet her there. During the service, I heard about the Shekinah Glory of God, which I had not heard before. After the service, I spoke to the pastor who explained that Shekinah means heavy. I shared my story of how God moved me to Arizona, of my closeness with God and the heaviness that comes upon me when I'm in His presence, and he confirmed I was sensing the Shekinah glory. I was moved to tears as God continued to show me that I was on the right path.[46]

I reflected back to a sermon by Dr. Tony Evans, *Start Your Day with God*, I listened to in February 2022. It was about connecting the "what" and the "why," from Luke 5:1-11. It was about Peter becoming a fisher of men. I heard a similar message around the same time by T.D. Jakes, though I didn't record the title of that sermon.

"So it was, as the multitude pressed about Him to hear the word of God, that He stood by the Lake of Gennesaret, and saw two boats standing by the lake; but the fishermen had gone from them and were washing their nets. Then He got into one of the boats, which was Simon's, and asked him to put out a little from the land. And He sat down and taught the multitudes from the boat.

When He had stopped speaking, He said to Simon "Launch out into the deep and let down your nets for a catch."

But Simon answered and said to Him, "Master, we have toiled all night and caught nothing; nevertheless at Your word I will let down the net." And when they had done this, they caught a great number of fish, and their net was breaking. So they signaled to their partners in the other boat to come and help them. And they came and filled both the boats, so that they began to sink. When Simon Peter saw it, he fell down at Jesus' knees, saying, "Depart from me, for I am a sinful man, O Lord!"

For he and all who were with him were astonished at the catch of fish which they had taken; and so also were James and John, the sons of

Zebedee, who were partners with Simon. And Jesus said to Simon, "Do not be afraid. From now on you will catch men." So when they had brought their boats to land, they forsook all and followed Him." NKJV

One thing we need to realize is that Simon Peter was a businessman; a fisherman. He had business partners, James and John. As fishermen they would go out at night to fish, then sell the fish at the market. This was their livelihood. They understood their business. They understood that the fish come to the surface at night when it is cooler. Fish also feed in shallow water, so, it would make sense that Simon, James, and John would fish in the shallow water.

In the first verse we see the multitude of people pressing in on Jesus because they want to see Him. Imagine a bowl-shaped lake. The water is in the bowl, and it is surrounded by mountains. Jesus was on the beach near the water and hundreds, maybe thousands, of people were pressing in on Him. He couldn't talk to them that way, so He climbed into the boat and pushed out into the water. That bowl-shaped lake made a great amphitheater so His voice was projected, and the multitude could hear Him as He gave a message to the people. Then He gave specific instructions to Simon [later called Peter]: "Push out into the deep [not where fish are usually caught] and let down your nets [not at the time of day when fish were caught]."

Notice the word "nets" is plural. Jesus told him to let down his nets. Simon was reluctant but said he would do it. Then, he let down his net (singular). We can give Simon a break here. He had worked all night and caught nothing. Tired and frustrated, he was probably cleaning his big, heavy nets at the end of the night shift and just wanted to go home and sleep. But Jesus asked him to put his clean net back into the lake. I can imagine what it felt like to not understand why he was being asked to do something that seemed counterproductive, unorthodox, and unconventional. It felt crazy, I am sure! Nevertheless, he obeyed, at least partially. He put down his net and it filled with fish until the net was breaking! Perhaps, if he had put down his nets, he would not have ruined his net!

How many times do we only perform an act of partial obedience? We read the Bible but don't take time to pray. Or we pray but only in the car on the way to work, never taking time to bow our heads and give Him uninterrupted time alone with us. Or maybe we give Him uninterrupted time, but we spend it with our laundry list of prayer requests never taking time to adore Him, make confession of our sins, or thank Him for our many blessings. There are many ways we can be like Simon. This was a great lesson for me to realize that I need to be ALL in!

Dr. Evans also explained that there is a word of God and a word from God. In this passage, He gave a message to the multitude. That is like when we go to church or listen to a sermon online. The pastor is giving the congregation or viewers a message of God. But the word from God is the personal message we receive, and everyone might have a different take away from that. God is personal. Personally, I don't believe Pastor Rick knew when he was preaching the word **of** God through the Move Series, that I was receiving a word **from** God to move to Arizona.

God told Simon where to go (into the deep), what to do (let down his nets), and what to expect (a blessing). But it didn't make sense to Simon. Jesus told him to go to deep water (not where fish are caught), let down his nets (in the daytime, not at night), and expect a catch when they had fished all night and there were no fish!

Dr. Evans said we can know when there is a blessing on the horizon when all our efforts are unsuccessful and what He asks us to do doesn't make sense. That was exactly true for me. I had been to two churches in the past ten years where I felt my efforts were unsuccessful. I was also experiencing financial struggles, and it did not make sense for me to pack up and move to a state with a cost of living ten percent higher than where I lived.

But look what God did! He moved me to my sister's house. A house she had no intention or idea that she would be buying just months before. I could live in her beautiful home; she and my brother-in-law were not there! They were in a different state visiting family for three months! It didn't cost me anymore to be in Arizona than it did to be in Kansas. I would never imagine that could be true but look what happens when we obey God!

There is another important piece to recognize in this story. The Bible does not tell us what happened to all those fish these men caught. There were enough to nearly sink two boats! Remember, Simon was a fisherman and a businessman. Fishing was his trade. He had business partners. So, what did they do with all those fish? Nothing Jesus does is wasted. Therefore, I believe they took those fish to the market and sold them. Why? In chapter four, it mentions Simon Peter's wife and mother-in-law. He had a family to support. God did not just say, "Come follow me." He said, in essence, be obedient, push out into the deep, let down your nets, and I will bless you. Can you imagine one-on-one mentoring with the Messiah? I believe Jesus also blessed Simon Peter by providing financially for his family as well as for his mission trip to become a follower.

It would be out of character for Jesus to call someone to go and not provide the way. Our responsibility is to trust and obey Him and watch how He provides when we do! I am a prime example! I was in a position where I had nothing financially to fall back on. I had zero dollars. I did not know how this move would happen or how I would survive. But I got to Arizona, and I had my sister's beautiful house to live in; I was able to keep my job and work remotely. When we obey, step out in faith, and trust Him, He will provide a way for us to do what He has called us to do.

A Thousand Ways to Die in Arizona
Way #11: Mojave Rattler

Adult Mojave Rattlesnakes have enough venom in just one bite to kill ten adults. While found in parts of California, Colorado, and Utah, these highly venomous snakes are found in the entire state of Arizona. Naturally. Of course, only 40% of untreated bites lead to death.

I suppose the odds are in my favor. Get treatment immediately if bitten by a snake!

Snakes are mentioned in the Bible several times. Most students of the Bible recall the serpent in the Garden of Eden, or the story when Paul was bitten by a poisonous snake and shook it off into the fire, unharmed. Then there is the rod that Moses threw onto the ground that turned into a snake. It is important to know who the enemy is, his schemes for getting us off course, and the importance of pressing ahead, moving forward, allowing God to take us from weak to warrior, from disbelief to faith, from fear to obedience.

In the Reflection section, look up the noted scripture and discover how God uses the snake to teach us more about the world we live in.

REFLECTION

1. Have you ever risked everything to be obedient to God's call on your life? Scripture tells us there is a cost to obedience, and one of those costs is stepping outside of our comfort zone and taking risks.

2. After taking a risk to walk in obedience, what have you seen as one or two of the blessings of obedience?

3. Genesis 3:1a *"Now the serpent was the most cunning of all the wild animals that the Lord God had made."* In the second half of the verse, what did the snake ask the woman? (Genesis 3:1b *"Did God really say, 'You can't eat from any tree in the garden'?"*) Trying to twist God's words and confuse Eve was a great tactic. We should beware, because the father of lies, the devil, uses the same tactics today—because it still works so well! Can you recall a time Satan tried to trick you into sin?

4. Exodus 7:10 *"So Moses and Aaron went into Pharaoh and did just as the Lord had commanded. Aaron threw down his staff before Pharaoh and his officials, and it became a serpent."* Has God ever told you to do something that seemed ridiculous? Did you do it?

5. Matthew 10:16 *"See, I send you out as sheep among wolves. Be then as wise as snakes, and as gentle as doves."* This references back to Genesis 3:1. Re-read the verse above. What is one practical way you can "be as wise as snakes"?

6. 2 Corinthians 11:3 *"But I have a fear, that in some way, as Eve was tricked by the deceit of the snakes, your minds may be turned away from their simple and holy love for Christ."* We must be wise and diligent so that we are not confused when Satan twists God's Word and tries to make us believe things that are untrue. How can we make ourselves wise?

CHAPTER

17

Occupy

The Kansas City Royals training camp in Surprise, Arizona is only a little over an hour drive from my new home. I first began watching the KC Royals when I was in grade school because my oldest sister watched them. Sitting on the threadbare carpet in our tiny rental home, I would watch Cookie Rojas and Willie Wilson (Willie was the centerfielder and my favorite player) as my sister rocked in the old wooden rocker.[47] Seeing as I was in Arizona, I was excited to watch the Cactus league at training camp!

The game was fun. I watched my newest favorite player, Salvador Perez (catcher), and talked with the couple next to me, sharing my story. They were amazed. They shared that their son was a new pastor in Grandview Missouri, in the great Kansas City metro area. Because of that, they came to see the Royals to make the connection. We exchanged phone numbers. When I got home, I had an intense and unexplainable feeling in my chest. It was a real, physical feeling, but not one I could define; it was a spiritual fullness.

I called Racquel to share this with her, relaying it felt like something was about to burst out of me, and something big was about to happen. Later that evening, my friend from North Texas called and, during the conversation, she told me about a woman named Julie who was the godliest woman she's ever known. A woman who hears from God and who starts grassroots efforts when God tells her to, and they are always blessed. She explained that Julie felt led to start a 30-day devotional in April and my friend wanted me to be part of it. I emailed Julie and joined the devotional, which began the following day.

About a week later, our church hosted a Women's Prayer Breakfast. I had only been a member of the church for one month, but I was excited to go to the fancy hotel downtown and join 350 other women for prayer. The theme was YES, and the color was red. Arriving in my daughter's red pant suit and heels, I saw hundreds of women in every shade of red, huddled in groups, chatting excitedly while waiting for the doors to open. Once we were allowed inside, we took in the large marque lit up in white lights, spelling out the word YES, and surrounded by dozens of red and white balloons. Just past the photo station were several long tables covered in white linen cloths and boasting a cornucopia of breakfast items: bacon, eggs, potatoes, grits, sausage, biscuits, gravy, oatmeal, muffins in every flavor, pastries, berries, melons, grapes, coffee, tea, and juice.

Inside the double doors were about fifty round tables also covered in white linen. Each had a table number on a card holder in the centerpiece to help me locate table 21 where I was to be seated. Our keynote speaker, Rev. Dr. Danielle L. Brown, talked about saying YES to God and not living in fear. She spoke about being bold and leaning into Him. Listening to her preach and listening to the roomful of women sing praises together, made me feel blessed and at peace. Each speaker encouraged me to say YES to God and allow Him to show me the open doors He wanted me to walk through.

On the last day of Julie's devotional, she ended with a call to action. She read Numbers 11 where 70 elders were raised up and she felt like she was supposed to raise up 70 city leaders to duplicate what she was doing in Dallas, which was training and equipping women to share the gospel at home and abroad to unreached people groups. She asked a simple question: "Will you say yes to more information?"

Staring at my computer screen I read, "Would you say **YES** to more information?" I moved my mouse to hover over the word, 'YES.' I said out loud, "It is the year of YES, so" (while simultaneously clicking the link) "yes, I will."

Julie and I had a Zoom call shortly after that. She told me about the organization and explained to me what being a city leader meant. She told me how I could be on staff. She told me about the last short-term mission trip where they had laid hands and prayed over many for healing and watched as God healed a paralytic, a blind man, and others. I wept. With genuine care and concern in her eyes and her voice, she asked what was going on. Hoping she did not think I sounded crazy, I told her all the things I had gone through and everything God was telling me. I told her how I watch a lot of sermons and take a lot of notes. Recently, God kept bringing the word *healing* to me. It would have nothing to do with the sermon I was listening to, so I would write the word with a question mark behind it.

She didn't think I was crazy. She said, "Yes, that is what we do. We heal in the name of Jesus!" As I shared my story with her and got to the part about God telling me to write a book, she didn't flinch. She took a note and casually said, "Ok, I have someone for that." My head was about to explode! Was this really happening? Wow. I was so overcome with God's goodness and faithfulness.

Julie works for an international ministry in the division called Arise, which is a women's ministry. The name comes from Song of Songs 2:10, *"Arise, my dearest. Hurry, my darling. Come away with me! I have come as you have asked to draw you to my heart and lead you out. For now is the time, my beautiful one."* (TPT)

Astounded

Completely astounded at all that had taken place in such a short amount of time, I decided to go through my journals and count how many times I had written the word, *healing*. What I found caused me to fall on my face before God and weep.

Between January and March, before I knew about Julie, I had written,

> "I will arise. Speak, pray, lay hands in the name of Jesus. 70 elders. Who's on my team? Full time ministry. Am I going to heal people in the name of Jesus? God blesses by funding His purpose. Healing. Pray for peace in the city of Phoenix. It is time to tell the world. God calls you to lead people. Heal the sick. Go where God called you to go. Healings? I need a team of women. Arise, preach, heal. I need a team of 4-5 women. Arise and Go. Healings was written over and over again – eight times.

God had told me He was sending me somewhere for a reason. I had more cause than ever to believe Him. I had prophesied over myself and did not even know it!

Julie came to Phoenix to meet with me and some other ladies from church to see if this was something we could launch in our area. At the end of the weekend, she suggested I make sure it was a God-call, because she knew He had used OCJ kids in answer to my prayers and she didn't see how the two ministries could intersect.

That Sunday I went to church and breathed a silent prayer. *Lord, speak to me today and let me know for sure if this is the right way.*

As I finished praying, the choir, all dressed in shades of yellow, sat in unison, and the pastor made his way to the wooden podium on the stage. He had his thick leather Bible opened and before he said anything else, he read from Jeremiah 18:4, "Arise and go…" That was all I needed. I looked up toward heaven and said, "Thank you!"

I didn't know yet how OCJ played into this, but I had no doubt what God was telling me to do. He can be trusted. All the answers were not clear. Things didn't make sense. Understanding is not required. I did not know how OCJ would intersect, but God did. And in the days that followed, they intersected pretty quickly!

While meeting with the director of Thrive Arizona about starting a Bible study on their campus for aged-out foster youth, the answer came. They were excited and welcoming, but said, "In order to be on campus, you have to go through training, and we do that training through OCJ Kids Ministry. I'm sure my mouth hung open in wonder at God's orchestration of this. They also told me about a coffee shop and thrift store they were opening and invited me to host Bible studies there, as well. That way I could get to know people in the area and pray with others.

Later, I read Jeremiah 18:2 to see what the rest of the verse said. "Arise and go down to the potter's house, and there I will let you hear my words." I went to Dallas for training a few weeks later and made my way back to The Potter's House on a Sunday morning. Seated next to my friends, I studied the expansive stage while expectantly waiting to hear from the Lord. When Sarah Jakes Roberts announced the title of her sermon, I sat in delight and disbelief. *"Arise, Go."* Her message was from Judges 7:9-18 about Gideon. She said, "I have to become. I can be in this city, I have no friends, but I'm becoming, and I have an audience. You are in that church to become. Move forward. He is making you a warrior."

Sarah Jakes Roberts reminded me who the enemy is and what I have to do to stay the course. Skillfully, the Holy Spirit spoke through her to my heart. Giving up is not an option. God WILL supply ALL the need. The vision is anointed. Walk in it!

He didn't send me to Arizona to die. He sent me to Arizona to bring life. To train and equip women to share the gospel to the nations. To answer my long forgotten prayer from forty years earlier. Send me.

A Thousand Ways to Die in Arizona
Way #819. Car Wrecks

Automobile accidents can happen anywhere, but I have seen more in Arizona than I ever saw in Kansas City. The wrecks here always seem to be major and shut down highways for hours. I did some searching on Google and discovered Arizona is sixth on the list of states with the most car wrecks. People on bicycles or walking are especially at risk. Always be on the lookout.

The sermon from 2021, *From Comfort Zone to Danger Zone* mentioned in chapter 5, really got to me and was the push I needed to move forward in seeking God's plan. Familiarity is my comfort zone, but Arizona highways seem to be a danger zone. I, too, wanted to stay in Kansas to be close to everything familiar, but God had another plan. He moved me 1,200 miles away – not because He didn't love me, but because He did love me and He wanted me to experience more of Him, grow my faith, and place me in ministry I would have never stepped into if I had stayed in my comfort zone. Car wrecks do happen, and they are probably mostly accidental. But stepping into the center of God's will and plan will always demand intentionality and obedience on our part.

The miracles and the words from God continue every day. He overwhelms me with His presence as I search for Him with my whole heart. He has shown me that working with aged out foster youth, especially young women, is my call for Arizona. Why I need to do it in Phoenix may always be a mystery, but God has a good plan, and I do not question it. Obedience is better than sacrifice, but sometimes, obedience requires sacrifice. I know one thing. He is worth it.

PROLOGUE

I cried a lot throughout this journey. I was so overwhelmed and overpowered by His presence, His Shekinah glory, which is very real. It's heavy, but not in the sense of being a burden. It begins at my head and then moves down my body, enveloping me in a sort of Spanx feeling, snug and hugging my body, but it is not uncomfortable. It is an actual, physical, literal sensation that captures my attention immediately and is so overpowering it causes me to be speechless and to simply fall on my face and worship Him. There is literally nothing else I can do in those moments.

I have seen God heal me from my childhood abuse and trauma and have been working on my anxiety and all issues that come from that sort of foundational pain. And I no longer have that awful fear of the future. God is my new foundation, and He holds me secure in who I am and my purpose in life. I have to remind myself that life is a journey, and the destination comes in the next life. We are called to obedience step by step.

Normally my life is probably much like yours. I pray and I wait for His timing and His answers. However, since the fall of 2021, it has not been so. I have prayed and immediately He answers me. Time after time and day after day He answers me in miraculous ways the instant I pray. And that is a tremendously emotional feeling. That's because, I believe, in learning to hear His voice and walk in obedience, my prayers reflect what He desires. Scripture says when we pray according to His will, He answers. And I rest in knowing that He is faithful, He provides for His children, and He guards our path. When we walk in obedience, we can know that God goes before us to lead the way and behind us as our rear guard.

In November 2023 a young pastor from a local church was sharing the gospel when someone opened fire. As I write this, he lies in a hospital bed fighting for his life. He is a person. A father. A husband. A friend. A pastor. A child of the Most High God.

When God called me to the mission field of Arizona, it did not seem too extreme. It's in America after all. I didn't have to learn a new language, the rules of the road, or how the government works. The food is the same and shopping is routine. While the culture is different and my driving skills have been sharpened due to the nature of the traffic, it is not a huge adjustment in comparison to those who are called to small villages on the other side of the globe.

That being said, knowing that sharing Christ's message with others is cause for harm is sobering. It is true that 90% of persecuted Christians live in Nigeria where one in six is killed for their faith in Jesus. Still, persecution of Christians in the United States is at an all-time high. Worldwide, one in seven Christians are persecuted with imprisonment, violence, or death. That is a high statistic.

The realization is that tomorrow is not promised. I want to tell as many people as possible about the saving grace of Jesus while I can. Yet, I understand the painful truth is that most people don't want to hear this message. Some ignore me, some make fun of me, and some do not understand me. Jesus warned us. He was beaten, He was treated badly, He was poked fun at. He was run out of town. He was hung naked on a cross. So, some may try to shoot me, and yet, I must use my voice and speak the truth while there is time.

God is amazing. The stories I have about the miracles I have seen will have to be in another book. The purpose of this book has been accomplished. I hope and pray I have inspired you to seek God and not fear obedience to Him. There may be a thousand ways to die in Arizona, but there is only one way to live, and that is for Him.

Not "The End."
Only "The Beginning...."

ABOUT THE AUTHOR

Jennifer Jaye is a missionary, speaker, and author. She is the founder of A Great Commission Ministry, a multimedia platform that trains and equips women to share the gospel in their home, their city, and around the world. Through podcasts, online content, prayer groups, and various other resources, A Great Commission Ministry seeks to unite, encourage, and prepare women to share their testimony boldly in order to impact both the physical and eternal lives of others.

She and her husband, Howard, are members of Pilgrim Rest Baptist Church in Phoenix, Arizona where they reside. There they are involved with the Outreach Team. They also volunteer with several foster care and homelessness organizations. Jennifer also hosts a YouTube channel called Movingforward1265. To date, her podcast has been viewed in 68 countries and translated into 17 languages. With her easy smile and simple messages, she is quickly gaining popularity.

Jennifer was born in Topeka, Kansas and raised in Lawrence, Kansas. She is a graduate of MidAmerica Nazarene University in Olathe, Kansas. She has four children and five grandchildren.

Scan this QR Code for Jennifer's YouTube channel.

CHAPTER

RESOURCES

Some of those words of encouragement are listed below. I hope these will be an encouragement and inspiration to you, as you seek to follow His will and discover His plan and purpose for your life.

1. Change is coming. He's doing new things. Find your purpose. (Pastor Rick George)

2. Be faithful and obedient to what God calls you to do. (Pastor Rick George)

3. God is preparing to throw something your way. (Pastor Rick George)

4. Out of nowhere comes a calling. (Pastor Rick George)

5. Something, a big assignment, a new call, is coming. (Pastor Rick George)

6. When God tells us to do something, we're going to do it until He tells us not to do it anymore. (Pastor Rick George)

7. Quit holding on to what's holding you back. Excuses are self-imposed limitations. (Pastor Rick George)

8. God always has a way forward. You just have to keep moving. (YouVersion 01/01/2022)

9. The inner me becomes the enemy because the inner me has the voice of the enemy (Pastor Andy Addis)

10. If you're stuck in your present circumstances, remember the past. Remember what God has done. Stop being afraid. Instead

of focusing on fear, focus on the things God has done in the past. Always remember and never forget. (Pastor Andy Addis)

11. God is going to do the unexpected. It won't be normal. It won't be routine. It will be more than you could ask or imagine or even think. (T.D. Jakes, 1/16/2022).

12. You have to move into a completely different dimension. A Kingdom dimension will change your life. Don't go back to the familiar because that's a lie. Don't stay there. This is the Lord's doing. (T.D. Jakes, 1/16/2022).

13. God made your mouth. If He has empowered you, you cannot fail! Don't believe the lies. (Francis Chan, May 3, 2013)

14. You are being prepared. Whatever the enemy means for evil, God means for good. (Antoinette Staples)

15. When God calls you, you have to go. You can't revoke it.

16. Expect a blessing, look for it, activate the plans of God. Do something with the time you've been given. God brought you here on purpose. God has plans for you. (Dr. Marcus Crosby, PRBC)

17. Keep moving! There's a blessing in the pressing. (Dr. Terry E. Mackey, PRBC)

18. You must be willing to be unorthodox. Be willing to be odd and be different. (T.D. Jakes)

19. You don't know what's next. You are going to be taken away from the familiar to get to know who you are. (T.D. Jakes)

20. Do what God calls you to do, you can't opt out of change; it's a learning season. (T.D. Jakes)

21. God is putting you in a situation that is too big for you, but that doesn't mean it's not yours to do. (T.D. Jakes)

NOTES

Introduction

1   John 8:44

Chapter 1

2   I have learned about my mother's life through the details between me and my siblings who all remember things a bit differently. The full truth is most likely buried with Mama.

3   This is not what the book is about, but it plays a vital role in my history and how I became who I am despite Satan's best efforts to silence me and take me out early.

4   As if she had any idea what she was looking at.

5   Here's my "Rock Chalk Jayhawk Go KU!" I attended KU and I am a huge fan!

Chapter 2

6   Eric R. eventually became a preacher and evangelist. He currently works with a ministry whose mission is to connect the citywide body of Christ to maximize kingdom impact. They share the gospel in the streets of Kansas City, Missouri, and send teams on short-term international mission trips to share the gospel of Jesus worldwide. You can find out more about this mission at thesendingproject.org.

7   I thank God daily for answering my prayer beyond what I could have asked or imagined. I was saved 2 ½ years later. My son, Eric, not only serves God but was blessed with a godly wife who adores him.

8   I was also confused about baptism. In the Catholic faith, babies are sprinkled on the forehead, which had already been done. But as I learned about baptism by immersion, I was obedient to God's call and followed Him in believer's baptism.

Chapter 3

10 Check him out on YouTube or Facebook.

Chapter 4

11 I was on the Finance Team, Missions Team, AWANA Director and teacher, Sunday School teacher from pre-K through Jr. High, including Special Ed, Nursery Coordinator, VBS Director.

12 https://www.friendshipcircle.org/blog/2010/10/13/autism-moms-stress-like-soldiers-families-bring-strength#

13 I see now that I wasn't seeking Him in the same way as before.

14 After high school I had attended the University of Kansas, but I majored in skipping class and day-drinking, so I dropped out.

15 NLCC 01/26/2020 Lucas Motley

Chapter 5

16 I joined social media in 2009 to stay connected to people both near and far! God had bigger plans for my interest in being on social media!

17 These sermons can be found at NewLifeGardner.com. Simply hover over Media and then click on Past Series.

18 Genesis 6-9

Chapter 7

19 Advent: The Journey to Christmas. A Church of the Highlands Devotional. YouVersion Bible App, December 2018

Chapter 9

20 Incidentally, I also did some research. I kept hearing the church service called Watch Night and I didn't know what that meant. I discovered that while President Lincoln signed the Emancipation Proclamation in September 1862, it didn't go into effect until January 1, 1863. "The Emancipation Proclamation freed slaves in the Confederate States during the American Civil War and is still celebrated on New Year's Eve in many African American churches."

21 I encourage you to use the YouVersion app for Bible studies, alone or with friends. You can have prayer partners, share prayer requests, and listen to the verse of the day, along with commentary on the verse. It's a great tool to grown, learn, and connect with others.

22 The week prior, Pastor Rick George from my home church in Kansas, New Life Community Church, had said, "God has a plan, and He will finish what He started."

23 Pastor Addis was on the leadership team of the Southern Baptist Convention, but I knew him from my original home church that I left after 23 years. He also served as the speaker of our second annual Back 2 Skool Bash.

24 Incidentally, he is still preaching and my great niece in Hutchinson, Kanas is now enjoying his youth events!

25 I suggest writing down the things God has done as you recall them. When you are fearful, go to that list. Add frequently answered prayers. Always remember and never forget. This will help you and future generations as they read your testimony.

26 You can listen to Pastor Martin's excellent sermons on YouTube or FaceBook at Greater Archview Baptist Church Little Rock.

Chapter 10

27 Apologies here to Bishop Jakes! I know who you are now, and God used you in a mighty way in my life.

28 In this book, T.D. Jakes uses the stories of women of the Bible to teach a different aspect of prayer. It's a great read and I highly recommend it.

29 Later on, Pastor Mackey asked me why the band was called Cain. He thought it an odd name for a Christian band and seemed genuinely concerned about what I was listening to. He sat in the large leather conference room chair in his suit and tie and asked me to try and find out about that name. As I was leaving the building, I did a quick search on my smart phone to see what I could find out. The three siblings who make up the band share the last name, Cain. No evil notion or hidden messages; just their name.

30 The Commission song by Cain, Songwriters: David Blake Neesmith, Logan Cain, Carter Frodge, Taylor Matz, Madison Jonson, Producer Jonathan Smith, 2020

Chapter 11

31 .Antoinette S. Branch, "You're Being Prepared," https://youtu.be/s2TXEVxfBjw?feature=shared. Assessed 09/23/2024

Chapter 12

32 Jakes, T.D. When Women Pray, 10 Women of the Bile who Changed the World Through Prayer, FaithWords, 2020

33 The loneliness was awful, and it didn't feel good, but He said it would be like this and He said to hang on because the victory is coming.

34 In just the first three weeks of having the channel I had received multiple messages on text, DM, and email from viewers who had been encouraged.

35 He also told me I would write a book, which overwhelmed me even more.

36 Exodus 4:10-17

37 Jakes, T.D., *When Women Pray, 10 Women of the Bible Who Changed the World Through Prayer*, FaithWords. 2020. pg. 196

Chapter 13

38 Isaiah 52:12, "For the Lord goes before you, and the God of Israel is your rear guard."

39 Psalm 37:23-24

40 If you are not familiar with the Armor of God, you can read about it in Ephesians chapter 6 beginning at verse 11.

41 From his sermon entitled, Road Rage https://www.youtube.com/watch?v=sHIqDzKinfY Accessed 08/15/2024

Chapter 14

42 The first episode was posted in February 2022, and my goal was to post two new shows weekly. I didn't always meet that goal, but I kept at it.

43 Remember that nugget I told you to hold on to? This is it.

Chapter 15

44 International Church of Hong Kong, YouVersion app; Lent: One Voice

Chapter 16

45 When I moved to Arizona, I had no cell service or cable. My phone didn't work, and the cable wasn't installed yet. So, I sat alone in the quiet. Every once in a while, I would get a text or a phone call, but calls drop constantly. I couldn't use my apps, watch YouTube sermons, or listen to the radio. I would read the Word of God, write in my journal, review my study notes. So, if God wanted me to know who I am and who He is, He put me in a place to do that.

46 In part 5 of my YouTube series, I explain what it's like when I'm watching sermons and talking to God. I sense His presence, and it is real, heavy, coming down from the top of my head and enveloping me. It isn't a burden of heaviness; it's a fullness.

47 Mama repainted the rocker black to make it look nicer, but it still creaked with each backward motion.

www.ingramcontent.com/pod-product-compliance
Lightning Source LLC
Chambersburg PA
CBHW060930120626
46557CB00003B/936

She Said Yes...

AND IT MADE ALL THE DIFFERENCE!

Cheri Dixon

Table of Contents

Introduction

Cheri Dixon Consulting was created in 2023, after the unexpected death of a friend. I realized that I was dedicating most of my time to my career and not making myself my priority. It is sad, but it takes a tragedy like losing someone too early to realize that life is too short! As I turned 50, I knew I needed a change and began planning my future, which included making all my goals and dreams a reality.

My business started with a blog, which led to me being part of some amazing books. My blog morphed into a podcast, and then an online talk show. While realizing how much I missed working to build and grow schools, I set out to build my leadership and business development consulting agency, and this is how Cheri Dixon Consulting was born.

I focus on working with women, empowering them to realize the skills that are in them and to become the strong women they were born to be. My daughter has always been the driving force in all I do—I knew that I wanted her to have a strong female role model in life that could show her that anything is possible.

She Said Yes And It Made All the Difference

I have always been a dreamer. I know it all started when I put on my first "dress-up" clothes and high-heeled play shoes as a young girl, and I always knew that I wanted to live a big life. I didn't always see this being modeled growing up, but people in my world always told me that I could do anything I set my mind to, so I believed I could.

Life brought me challenges, big ones, just like it does for so many of you. But those voices from my past stayed on repeat as I went through every one of them, reminding me I could do anything, even when I lost belief for a moment. This book is my way of sharing those moments…times in my life when I had to make a choice that was hard and what I learned about myself during each one. Desire and faith are crucial in making your dreams a reality. I know I would not be where I am today without that relentless desire for a big life and the faith that it could become a reality. My hope is that as you read my story, you laugh, cry, and, most importantly, understand that when life gives us challenges, we have the power to say yes and make all our goals and dreams come true. If I can do it, you can, too!

This book could not have been one of my realities without the love, support, and encouragement of my circle. Thank you to She Rises Studios for seeing that I was meant for big things and for always supporting women. Thank you to my colleagues and mentors over the years who motivated me on my toughest days and cheered with me on the great ones. Thank you to my friends and family who have listened to me talk about this project during every conversation over the last year. And thank you to my daughter, my girl, my best friend. I love being your mom and you have taught me how to be the best version of me! To The Mommy-Baby Hood!

To all my readers, go be big!

My Courageous Resilience: Saying Yes to Life's Unexpected Path

W*riting a book has always been one of my dreams. I have had so many great opportunities in life and overcome just as many challenges, and I always believe that if we have knowledge or skills, we should always share them with others.*

Honestly, I did not really think this could be possible. And I'm not exactly sure how I became connected with the group of amazing women who made this dream a reality for me, but things happen for a reason and when I was asked to write my first chapter in an anthology, I had to say yes.

Over the past two years, my life has changed so much. I have reinvented myself a few times in my 52 years on this earth, but this last pivot has been a big one. I left a profession that I knew I was going to enter from a very young age. I left not because I didn't love it any longer, but because I knew it was time to focus on myself and make all of the crazy dreams I have had over the years become a reality. Life is definitely short, and I never want to live with regret!

My goal with this book, She Said Yes…And It Made All the Difference, *is to give each of you reading it hope that no matter what comes at you in life, no matter where you are from or the challenges you had as a child, you can make a big life a reality. Allow yourself to pursue your dreams! Give yourself permission to think big! Give yourself the grace to stumble as you learn new ways of living! We cannot expect to continue to do the same thing over and over in life and achieve different results. You simply must choose to make yourself a priority and say yes when those opportunities come along that will change you forever! Enjoy!*

I remember the moment in my life when I first understood the feeling of fear. My dad was driving us up Pike's Peak in Colorado Springs, where we lived while he served in the military. Seeing that mountain from the ground gives anyone the feeling of awe. It seemed to me like the mountain top reached the stars. I loved it! And I know my dad did as well. However, driving up that mountain, my cheek pressed against the window so I could see everything all the way down, completely overwhelmed me, and that was the moment I developed a fear of heights. I kept thinking about how if our car veered off just inches too far, we would fall off that mountain. As an adult, I now know that wasn't going to happen, but as a five-year-old, that feeling of fear overtook my world.

Fear continued to overtake my feelings throughout my childhood. I loved my teachers growing up. I've shared many times how I believed my teachers were superheroes, making the teaching profession seem like the most glamorous profession ever! But going to school each morning began with a feeling of dread. I was a victim of bullying, even before it was something parents, teachers, and children ever worried about. I was very quiet and shy and didn't engage in a lot of conversations with other students unless I felt very comfortable. I knew I was a bright child, and my classmates did as well. Sounds like a great thing unless you are someone who was made fun of due to your intelligence. And once I allowed my "bully" to know that her taunting bothered me, she went in 100%, ridiculing me in front of others as often as she could. Fear overtook my feelings once again and caused me complete embarrassment. As a matter of fact, I have not shared this with anyone until now, due to the fact that I have always felt that I was less than because I couldn't control what was happening.

Home is supposed to be your safe space. As the oldest child in my family, I felt that when my parents were present and we were all working together to be a close family, life was great and safe. Things in life change quickly, however. One day all is well, and another your mother has shown you a different side of her that takes the safe feeling away in an instant. It could have been when I learned my mother was having an affair, and of course, my dad had no idea. It could have been when she convinced me not to tell him because she knew she made a mistake and was going to end it, and telling him would tear our family apart. Or it could have been that time, after another argument we had about her adulterous behaviors, that ended with her on top of me, slapping me repeatedly in the face. But when your feeling of safety instantaneously turns to fear and takes over your entire being, that is when you truly understand the feeling.

Those close to me never questioned why I immediately became a perfectionist, a people pleaser, and someone who played life safe. I went to school on time, came home on time, studied hard, and ensured that I was a "good" girl so I could control my feelings of fear and stay under the radar, hidden from anyone who could possibly threaten my security. Those closest to me also never questioned my work ethic and drive, which allowed me a future that could take me away from the very environment that, in my mind, caused me to feel fear. It also didn't surprise anyone that I was looking for someone to love me. Throughout high school, I had dreams that I would meet my "man in shining armor" who was coming to rescue me, leading me to a life of eternal bliss. I dated…a lot. And knowing that I never give up on a dream, Prince Charming actually did show up!

I met him during my senior year of high school. We immediately connected and began building our future dream life. We had plans to go to college, become established professionals in our respective fields, and live a glamorous life. Children were not necessarily in that future plan. Why would someone who had endured so much pain and sorrow in her own relationship with her mother risk having children and one day become a replica of her? Not me. And that was the plan.

Here is the funny thing about life. It sometimes throws you curveballs. Yes, Prince Charming and I began a life together. The wedding was beautiful…everything I dreamed of as a young child. But it included our beautiful baby girl by our sides. And yes, we were now a family of three. Two teenagers playing house, trying to not let fear overtake every step of our lives. I now had the title of Mom…one I never imagined having; a role I never thought I could fulfill. Even the doctor who delivered her that night thought I may not be fit for the role and encouraged me to give her up for adoption so I could still make my future prosperous. The emotions swirled around inside me. Fear was consuming me.

But when I looked into her beautiful blue eyes on that warm August night in the hospital after the experience of childbirth, I knew I had to say yes…and it made all the difference.

CHAPTER 2

Overcoming Childhood Fear and Designing My Future

How many times have you had a conversation with someone and they tell you that they cannot do a certain thing because they had a bad childhood? Or maybe you doubt your own capabilities because of past experiences and never allow yourself to pursue your big dreams in life.

I am a huge fan of '90s grunge music. After spending time with me, you would quickly realize Nirvana is one of my favorite bands (have you seen the cover of this book?). I love that this era of music was raw and artists were authentic, putting their experiences out there to share with the world. I also felt a connection with so many of these artists, as I too could have written or sung about the many hurdles in my own life that seemed to continually show up. We are a sum of all of these past experiences combined. They give us our personality. They give us our voice. They direct how we show up in life. Listening to just one Nirvana song, anyone could tell that Kurt Cobain also endured many hardships growing up. And how did his life end? Way too early…as he couldn't get past his own hurdles, and it ended in one of the worst ways.

Life is hard. Even when we think people have it all together, many are battling demons from their past. And if we can't get control and realize that our only remedy is focusing on our future and moving forward, we all could fall into the trap of similar experiences. Maybe not quite so final, but life-ending in other ways.

My experiences growing up had a huge influence on who I am as an adult, but I did not allow those experiences to determine my future. I learned that we all have hurdles in life. How we handle them and continue to move forward, creating a life we want to live, is the key to moving past the hurt, the fear, and the trauma of those experiences.

What I haven't shared is that while I was growing up and dealing with all the challenges that came to me, I also had big goals and dreams that I wanted to accomplish. I wanted to be a professional woman who wore suits and fabulous high heels each day at my job. That job was in the realm of public education, where I would build a reputation for educating students so they could build their dream lives and support my colleagues with collaboration and strong networks. I planned to marry one of those models on the cover of GQ, and not only would I live in the most amazing home on a golf course, but also drive a red Corvette. I would accomplish this all while still building meaningful relationships with others and making a big impact on the world.

Did I accomplish all those dreams? I wore business suits, and yes, they were always accompanied by a pair of fabulous high heels each day, only after I worked full time and went to school full time to get my degree, even while mommy duties waited for me at home. I became the valued authority in education, as I taught some of the most challenging students on the east side of Houston, eventually working my way into the principal role and extending my influence to include supporting and growing teachers. I married that handsome Prince Charming I met in high school. He wasn't a GQ cover model, but he was handsome nonetheless. As a strong single woman, I not only found a neighborhood with a beautiful golf course to call home but went on to be able to actually build my own dream home that is designed and decorated in a way that lets the world know that Cheri Dixon lives here. And that red Corvette? Well, I don't have it yet, but the shiny black Lexus in my garage looks pretty good. But most importantly, with the work I do, I'm on a mission to directly impact 5,000 women in the next 10 years. I have seen many women sparkle and shine when they realize that with my support, they can build a life they love.

Why do I share this? Yes, I am proud of all that I have accomplished, but that is not my why. I share because if this girl, who endured the hurdles she has in life, can make her goals and dreams come true, so can you.

The first big lesson I learned by saying yes was that my past does not define me. Yes, it made for some challenges and some of those feelings of fear creep back up for me from time to time. I cannot control what life brought to me growing up, but I can control how I respond and the future I want to build for myself.

Desire and faith were two more feelings I learned early in life. I desired to make my dreams a reality. Not just sort of wanted them to come true, but thought about them every minute of every day.

I posted them on sticky notes, all around my space, as a constant visual reminder. I set goals with detailed plans. My desire was relentless. It pushed me forward when times were hard and wouldn't let me give up.

Part of this lesson was to not only have the desire but to have faith. I had to believe that I could accomplish these goals. I had to have the faith that I was strong enough to endure hard times and overcome them. I had to know that if I couldn't figure it out, I had people around me who would listen and support me along the way.

The day I met my daughter, with her bright red hair and inquisitive blue eyes looking at me for love and guidance as she started her own life, I knew I had to let go of my fear, let go of the past, and begin building a life for us. One that showed her what a strong woman was. One that taught her that our past does not define us. One where she felt love and support each day of her life, and that taught her that when fear crept in, she had the tools to overcome that fear and make her dreams a reality.

I said yes…and it made all the difference!

Real-Life Application

1. Do you need to let go of things from your past? We know that everything that has taken place in our lives has made us who we are today. We can't change the past. But we can design our own future. To do so, we must remember that our focus needs to remain on what is ahead. Choose one or two things that continue to control your life from your past. Focus on letting them go. Visualize yourself as someone who has overcome the hurt or betrayal from the incident. What do they look like? How do they live life? What lies ahead in their future? Now, go be that person. Stay focused on what you can control, and on what lies ahead.

2. Reflect on your life. What are some of the big goals and dreams that you had over the years that fear stopped you from pursuing? Choose 10 items from your bucket list that, if there were no limits, you would want to accomplish. Write them down. Then ask yourself, *What is stopping me today from pursuing these dreams?* Is it a lack of relentless desire? Is it because you don't have faith that these things could become a reality? Choose one or two items from your list that you would like to focus on making a reality. What do you need to do to make this happen?

CHAPTER 3

Embracing the Unknown: Saying Yes to My Dreams Amidst My Fear

I knew I was going to be a teacher at six years old. I truly believed that all my teachers were superheroes. Not only did they support me and build my desire to learn all I could and, in turn, have a huge impact on the world, but I also thought they made the profession look so amazing. Who didn't want to wake up each day, put on fabulous professional clothes, and go help children realize they could do anything they wanted in life? That is how I saw my teachers!

College was challenging. Not because I couldn't do the work, but because as a mom, wife, full-time student, and full-time employee, I had to learn how to schedule my time, prioritize all of the tasks, and juggle family responsibilities. It was well known in my small town in north Iowa in the early 1990s that finding a teaching position was very difficult. So not only did I need to do mommy, wife, and employee duties to the best of my abilities, but I had to stand out in my studies so that when the time came, I would do the impossible…get the dream job at one of the local schools where I had roamed the halls as a student myself!

With my degree in hand, I attended my first teacher job fair! I cannot even describe the excitement I felt! I knew going in that I was probably going to be approached by every school administrator there that was hiring…because yes, I thought I was that good! It turns out, job fairs don't quite work that way. I met a lot of people hiring, handed out a lot of resumes, and even got a couple of job offers. Not one of those offers was in my hometown…not even in my home state! I kept telling myself, you can't seriously think about accepting this. You have a home, a family, your husband has a job. My dream of actually becoming a real teacher was coming to a screeching halt, fast! I realized I had wasted a lot of blood, sweat, tears, and money to finish college and get that degree. I started to believe I was going to become a highly qualified daycare owner…fearing that would be my future.

Then I met Don (I changed his name for this story, and you will soon see why). Don became my stalker. Not really, but all of a sudden, while I was gathering my thoughts and emotions that day, wandering around that large, crowded venue, Don approached me like he had known me all my life as he leaned in and said, "You don't want to accept any of these jobs. These people are a bit crazy."

It turned out, Don was a principal at a school on the east side of Houston, Texas. And I also learned, while he followed me around, working hard to convince me to take a position with him, that his best friend was the principal at the small but wonderful school where I had completed my student teaching. That principal saw huge potential in me, and although he didn't have any openings, he knew I should be in a classroom making a difference for children. Don offered me a fifth-grade reading teacher position in Houston.

On the inside, I wanted to jump up and down, telling the world I just got the job of my dreams (if only it were close to home)! But in reality, I had to thank him and let him know I could not accept this position because I could not uproot my family to move 1,000 miles from home. He understood, and as I made my way back to my car, I realized that fear was once again showing up in my world.

During my drive home, I kept reasoning with myself. Why couldn't I take the job? Because that wouldn't be fair, to change everyone's world just so I could teach. What if we went and it created so many great opportunities for us…but what if we went and I failed, leaving us in a tougher place than we already were? What if…and then I forced myself to put it out of my mind. I could "what if" all day long, and I knew myself; I would let fear win every time. I did not believe I was strong enough or brave enough to venture away from my comfort zone and try something new. I resolved that I could substitute teach, tutor students, or work at a daycare to earn enough money to pay the bills. One day the dream of teaching in my own classroom would come true, but that day was not today.

I continued with my normal life during the next two weeks. Sure, I shared my experience at the job fair with my husband, family, and friends, but I ended each of those conversations the same way. I couldn't be selfish and uproot my family and move 1,000 miles away without my safety net, my support system. Yes, fear was now dominating my conversation. Deep down, I knew I could, but the fear of failure won each time. However, it was an unusually warm day in May when I got a life-changing phone call.

My husband was off work that day and answered the phone. He called me into the room and told me that Don was on the phone and wanted to propose an idea. As I spoke to him, he explained that I really shouldn't turn down his job offer without at least seeing the school. He offered to let me visit the school and promised to also provide me with great sightseeing opportunities around the amazing city of Houston. He got me when he asked if I'd ever been to Houston, and I realized I hadn't traveled more than four hours away from my small town in all of my adult life…and neither had my husband. So, we agreed. We would just go see the school and the city. I mean, we had been to Minneapolis before, and I was sure Houston couldn't be much different than that!

We drove to Houston over Memorial Day weekend. The farther south we went, the hotter it became. By the time we hit Dallas, we both looked at each other and wondered what we had gotten ourselves into. So many freeways (I'm not sure we even understood what a freeway was before this experience). So many cars and people. So many huge buildings. I tried to control his (and my) fear by saying, "I'm sure Houston is not like this at all."

We made it to the north part of Houston…and an hour later, after endless traffic, road construction, and miles upon miles of city…we made it to our destination, the east side of Houston. I know neither of us realized we were going to the fourth-largest city in the United States. Before parking the car, I already answered the fear's voice in my head…no, city life is *not* for me.

The school tour was amazing, however, and I once again realized that teaching definitely was my dream. Scared or not, Houston or someplace else, I needed to be in the classroom. The sightseeing around the area added to my excitement. We even saw the ocean! I kept thinking about my childhood dream…marry Prince Charming and live a big life. I began to wonder if that big life was in this big city!

We drove back to our small town and talked about every moment of our Houston trip. My husband started the questions. Did you like the school? I loved it! Did you like the people? Oh yes, so friendly and helpful! And then the big one…Do you think we can do this? I wanted to say yes…but here came fear again…and I said, I don't know. It's a lot of change. We will have to be here alone. It is hot. We have a home that we would have to sell. What would you do for work? The conversation ended with my resolve that I could sub, tutor students, or work at a daycare to pay the bills.

Memorial Day weekend is also my birthday weekend. And in my family, everyone gathers for everyone's birthday. As we rolled into our small town, we didn't head home.

We went straight to my dad's for my birthday celebration. We walked in and everyone had questions! How was it? Did you see the ocean? Was there traffic? Are you moving? I know that one was everyone's most important question. I told them that maybe Houston wasn't for us, but we were still working on our decision. Easy right? You would think, until someone said, "Yes, it was probably a wasted trip. You can't move there. You can't live without family!"

My husband looked at me, turned to my family, and said, "Actually we are putting the house on the market tomorrow. We are moving to Houston."

The group looked to me for my response. I felt so many emotions at that moment! My heart was saying yes! My head was saying, WTF! Teaching my own class was my dream, but leaving my comfort zone was scary. I wanted to go, but I was terrified. I never imagined in all of my life that I would be making a decision like this that would affect so many. The perfectionist, people-pleaser that I was took over! I didn't want to upset my family by being the first person among us to leave our small town. I didn't want to upset my husband and not seem like we were in agreement with our decisions. And then there was that beautiful baby girl, who was now almost five and preparing to start kindergarten. I wanted her at that wonderful neighborhood school, making life-long friends and excelling in all she did!

Then I felt a bit of anger. I was put on the spot to make a life-changing decision within seconds, and I was not sure I was ready to do so. That job would be fabulous, but I began to doubt if I could really do it. But I had to respond…they were all anxiously waiting.

I said yes…and it made all the difference!

CHAPTER 4

Listening to My Inner Voice on My Path of Change

Have you ever moved 1,000 miles from home during the month of August, transitioning to a tropical climate? We loaded our moving truck on the last Friday in July of 1995 to make our big move. It was hot in my small north Iowa town that day, but nothing compares to a summer day in Houston, Texas. We arrived late in the night, and we were already sweating from the heat and humidity.

Our house sold within a week of being on the market…definitely a sign that this was the right decision. By the time we pulled out of town to make the long journey, my family's anger shifted to worry with a little excitement sprinkled in. Most of the family already had plans to visit over the next six months! Another sign that this was the right move.

Our new apartment was pretty amazing and included a swimming pool, which is standard for Houston apartments, but considered a luxury where we come from. Our daughter already had a schedule prepared to practice her swimming each day after school, at "her" pool. Another sign.

With so many things looking good regarding this move, there were still some hurdles. These hurdles definitely made fear creep up for me again. The amount of traffic seemed daunting, and I was not very confident that I was going to learn how to navigate it successfully. Every few miles along any route in a city brings a completely different neighborhood, with a different culture, and a variety of residents. My route to and from school was no different, making me worried about our safety at times. And although I was walking into my dream job, my husband had no idea what he would do for work and didn't have the credentials to get a job he could choose. I was going to be the sole income earner as we made our start in this big city, and my income was only that of a teacher in the 1990s…definitely not one that was going to afford us the luxuries in life!

Looking back on this experience, however, it was the best decision we ever made as a family. I was going to be able to teach in my own classroom at a school where I would form bonding relationships with my colleagues, some stronger than those with my own biological family and still strong to this day. My husband did find work and eventually got to a place where his company saw the value in what he could offer and, over the years, our financial struggles became less of a hurdle. Our daughter started kindergarten, fortunate to be at the same school as I was. By the time she left fifth grade, she had a wonderful group of friends, a solid academic foundation, and had found her passion for helping others and her love for theater arts, which would set her up for so much future success.

I did not start my teaching career as a fifth-grade reading teacher, but as a fourth-grade math teacher. Understanding mathematics is a gift of mine, and I was now fortunate to teach it to others and help them build a love for the wonderful world of math.

Once again allowing myself to say yes, even when I was terrified, I continued to learn a valuable life lesson. One of the biggest lessons, which I continue to remember even now, is that it is ok to listen to your inner voice. During this transition, my inner voice kept telling me that I could take this big leap. It kept reminding me that I was more capable than I believed. It was giving me permission to let my dream of teaching become a reality. Some call it your intuition, and however we refer to it, I learned that when that inner voice speaks, I need to listen.

Our mind is our most powerful tool. If it tells us we can or can't, it is always correct. As an avid half-marathoner, I know that gearing up for the 13-mile run requires training. I map out my running schedule, increasing the miles of my long runs each week. I develop a strength training routine that keeps me strong but doesn't overdo it, preventing future injuries. I adjust my diet and sleep schedules so that I can run the miles and still stay healthy and able to live my active life. With all of this planning and preparation, one would think that every week's training would go smoothly, and all the miles would be easily completed.

As I mentioned, however, the mind is a powerful tool. Even with the best-laid plans, there are times when I struggle to complete the training because my mind starts to tell me that I am tired, or it convinces me that I am bored. And worse yet, it yells out that these runs are just too hard, and unless I can control it, I end up ending that run early and missing the miles.

Knowing when to listen to your inner voice is also very important.

When times are uncomfortable and you are struggling, don't let it convince you to quit. That voice is your fear. That voice does not want you to reach your goals and dreams. That voice may stop you from living your best life. But the voice that gives you permission to try, even when it seems impossible, is the one to get to know. Let that voice be your best friend, your cheerleader. That's the one that wants to see you succeed. It's that voice that will allow you to live a big life!

Change is hard. Most people stay stuck in a situation that may not be the best for them because they don't want to be uncomfortable. Even a bad situation that is familiar is better than the unknown of change. I learned that if we reframe our thoughts and begin to believe that change is actually an opportunity for something better, those better opportunities begin to come our way.

How many times have you heard someone complain about their life, indicating that it doesn't get better than this and they just need to accept it and deal with it? I think of the old Dunkin' Donuts commercial: The older gentleman is clearly not excited about getting up for work each day as he states, "Time to make the donuts," in the most monotone voice ever. We are not trees. If we are not happy with our life, or even just want more, we can do it. We can move in a different direction. We are not planted deep down in the ground, destined to stay in our current situations. However, we must remember that, although scary at times, change can bring so many new, amazing opportunities. I look at it this way—what do you have to lose? If it doesn't work, you gain experience and you can go back to where you were before. But what if it does work? What if it opens so many more doors? What if you get the chance to take the opportunity and it allows you to build your dream life?

My first year of teaching was a whirlwind. It started with a lot of unknowns, a lot of stress, and a lot of tears. As a matter of fact, I quit in my mind every day that first semester. But I dug deep, remembered my grit, and kept my "why," the dream of making a difference for children, as my daily motivation. Over the next five years as a classroom teacher, I found my path, perfected my teaching skills, built a network of other educators who helped me be better every day, and positively affected the lives of all of those students who came through my classroom door. My daughter was thriving in all areas of her life. My husband was building future success. We were truly on the path to living our big life in this big city!

I said yes…and it made all the difference!

Real Life Application

1. How do you handle your inner voice? Reflect on times in your life when you were presented with a big decision. How difficult or easy was it to make your decision? When determining your next steps, what was your inner voice telling you? And more importantly, did you listen? Was your inner voice your cheerleader or another hurdle in your path?

   Now, let's play a game. What if you only listened to your inner cheerleader when presented with that decision? Would that decision have been different? Would your entire life look different if you had focused more on the voice that gave you permission to take the next step in making your dream life a reality? Commit to listening to that voice when making scary decisions.

2. We all know that change is hard. That inner voice that keeps us stuck rears its ugly head and convinces us that it's more comfortable to stay in the familiar than it is to step into the unknown. Has this ever happened to you?

   Change can actually be an opportunity for positive outcomes which can open doors that will help you build your dream life. Next time you have an opportunity to try something new (even start with something small while you are starting this new way of thinking), take time to reflect on the positive effects this change could present for your life. Ask yourself if being uncomfortable for a while is worth these possibilities. Give yourself permission to take the first step!

CHAPTER 5

Redefining Success: Saying Yes and Accepting the Call to Lead

We were living life large those first years in Houston! Well, once we got past the first few hurdles of the first year in our new city. Yes, I said it…in our new city! Houston had become our new home. And we quickly realized we loved it! I almost felt as if we were part of one of those popular reality shows that highlight beautiful, young professionals living their glamorous lives. Add to the mix a couple with an elementary-aged child, and that was our life!

My teaching career was amazing…all that I had dreamed it would be! My students loved being in my classroom and each year they made so much progress. The families felt so happy when they learned that their child was assigned to my classroom and showered me with welcome gifts at the start of each new year. I worked with some of the best educators out there and we all supported and learned from each other every day. And I found myself being offered opportunities for so many great leadership experiences…heading up committees, leading my team, developing innovative programs to help our high population of second language learners at our school, and being a trusted parent partner with the other parents of my daughter's friends and classmates. I was truly making an impact!

My daughter was developing into her own wonderful being as well. She had a great group of classmates who continued to be her homeroom class each year, part of those innovative programs we created so that their advanced thinking and creative minds could be fostered year after year. She sang in the choir, learned to play piano, and built her love of performing. She started acting in plays, which became a love of hers and eventually landed her a college scholarship. She volunteered as often as she could right alongside me and really developed a heart for serving others, having her own impact on the world.

My husband was finding his way in this big city as well. Being a classic introvert, his idea of a big life was different from mine, but he found a job he enjoyed and made some friends that he, too, could call family. As a team of three, however, we all knew that we were lucky—fortunate enough to have found the courage to make this big move years prior and resourceful enough to build a life we loved.

About four years into my career, I was teaching third grade. Third grade had actually become my sweet spot. I loved the age group, found so many engaging ways to deliver the curriculum effectively, and had even been chosen to mentor student teachers assigned to our building. I had discovered my passion for working with our immigrant students, who were not only learning the required academic skills but also acquiring English as a second language. My principal knew my skill set, ensured I received any additional training, and allowed me to work with some of our lowest-performing students. Seeing them soar each year was a reward in itself, but that year seemed extra special. My students made more progress than I had ever seen. My student teachers were leaving me at the end of their assignments and securing every position they wanted. My colleagues began coming to me more and more for advice and support in their own classrooms. And my principal started pulling me in on different meetings when discussing plans for the whole school. I was becoming a valued and trusted educator who was not only impacting my assigned students but who had a hand in the success of the entire school building.

And then it happened. It was a beautiful sunny afternoon in March, the Friday before Spring Break. We were all excited about starting our break and looking for a few low-key activities for our students so that we could finish the day calmly and make our way to our weekly happy hour. Our principal came on the loudspeaker unusually early and told us she had a big announcement to make. And then…she announced that our Teacher of the Year had been selected…and it was me!

Now, I know how life is and that these awards can be based on popularity. But I also knew that I did become that valued and trusted teacher on campus, the one my colleagues wanted to choose for this award, and that meant a lot to me. I also knew that receiving this recognition would change the future of my career. When that is added to a resume, especially being at the school I was at (this campus was a highly regarded school in a highly effective district), people would take note. I was honored by the award, and I just kept hearing that inner voice say, *Yes…moving to Houston and allowing myself to teach in my own classroom was the right decision.* The rest of the year went just as I had imagined, with more people seeking advice from me, more parents eager to get their children in my classroom for the upcoming year, and me feeling more confident about my own skills. I had come a long way in these four years of being a teacher and could not even begin to think that I would choose to do anything differently because I was truly living the dream.

Summers go by fast! Yes, teachers have time off, but once you do some professional development, catch up on appointments for yourself and your child, and really clean your house (the struggle is real…but a story for another time), the time is gone, and you find yourself gearing up for all of the back-to-school festivities. The start of the year was smooth. My daughter was beginning her final year in elementary school, and I continued to teach my favorite grade level, third grade. My students and parents were amazing and, once again, I just knew I was living the dream!

The school year was moving along, and I had nothing to worry about! The students were learning and building a community within their classroom. I do believe this group could have been the best group of students I had ever had. I was teaching them how to describe in detail when writing when we were interrupted by a call from my principal. She told me that she was in the conference room with a few district administrators and needed me to join them. She said someone was on their way to cover my class and I should report to her immediately. I started frantically thinking…wow! Her tone was pretty serious. Had I done something wrong?

I sat down with her, three people from the district level, and my best friend, who had recently been promoted to instructional specialist for our campus. Yes, I was nervous, as I had no idea what was going on. Surely, if it was something good, my friend would have told me.

My principal started by saying that she could see how great my students were doing…ok, that is good. She said that each person in the room had noticed how much I had grown in the last year…also good.

And then she said it: "So, we are going to make a change to your current assignment. We want you on the administrative team. You will begin transitioning out of your classroom over the next couple of weeks. I have a replacement for you, who I will meet with today, and you can start training her as soon as tomorrow. We will tell your students and families on Friday. Your new assignment will be our campus Bilingual Instructional Specialist, working with our bilingual and ESL teachers and students. We will need to meet soon to discuss details and get you ready to start your master's program, but that can wait until next week. Congratulations! You are on your way to being one of our future principals one day soon! Do you have any questions?"

I sat there for a moment, trying to take this all in. I am sure I looked as confused as I was. I looked at my best friend, and she was smiling from ear to ear. Everyone at the table seemed extremely excited and ready for me to jump up and down with joy. And I should have been doing just that! But…

I thanked my principal and everyone in the room. I told them how honored I was that they chose me and that I would prepare for the transition, and of course, I would do my best in my new assignment. I finished the school day and shared the news with my husband and daughter during dinner.

When I finished the story, I looked at them both, and said, "But I think I'm going to go in tomorrow and say no. I love being in the classroom. I love my students. And what if I can't do this new job as well?"

My daughter's expression changed in a moment. She went from smiling, beaming with pride that her mama was chosen (even at this young age, she knew how much hard work I had put into developing my career), to disappointment that the fear was going to hold me back.

My daughter knew—fear was once again holding me back. All night I kept trying to talk myself into believing there was no way I could become an administrator. I wasn't ever going to be good enough to be a principal. I would never find the money to be able to go back to school and get my master's degree. These doubts just fed into the fear. The bottom line was that I was too afraid to take this big leap because I was sure I would fail. I was fully prepared to disappoint a whole lot of people when I told them that I loved being in the classroom and just didn't think I should leave my students this far into the year. My mind was set.

They say a new dawn can bring new hope! And as I was driving to school that next morning, I started to hear my inner voice begin talking to me again. Actually, it just started yelling! That cheerleader was definitely cheering me on, while fear's voice was still trying to hold me back. I began thinking, ok, I didn't know anything about teaching when I started, and my first year was horrible, but I figured it out. Look how far I have come. *Yes, but being an administrator…that is a big responsibility.* Ok, but what if I took the first step and committed myself to learning all I need to know? I am pretty responsible. *Well…how are you going to pay for that master's program?* I'd had no idea how I was going to get through college before, but I figured that out. *Ok…but now your daughter is heading to middle school and will be at a new school away from you. She will need you more.* Maybe she will, but she did seem very proud when I shared the news, so I am sure we can figure out schedules so that we will all be ok.

I finally looked in the rearview mirror before getting out of my car that morning and said…bottom line, you can stay in the classroom, comfortable with your 22 students, or you can take that next step and see just how many more students, families, and teachers you can impact in the future. It will be a challenge, but you can do hard things. Go live a big life!

I said yes…and it made all the difference!

CHAPTER 6

Building My Influence and Impact

The next couple of years were a whirlwind, and I have to admit, full of so many emotions. Leaving the classroom was a challenge. I missed my students and the structure that being a classroom teacher had provided me. The new position had been newly created, so it was like we were building the plane while we were flying it. Each week, each day, brought a new set of responsibilities, and navigating it was hard. However, I did have the opportunity to help develop this position, one that would truly affect so many students, and lay the groundwork for others who filled the role after me.

I found a way to go back to school and get started on my master's degree. The University of Houston had an opportunity for bilingual and ESL teachers who were interested in becoming school principals to apply for a grant that fully funded a master's program in Educational Leadership. The requirements to apply were quite rigorous, making me wonder if I would ever meet the mark. However, I needed this degree to move forward in my career, so although hesitant, I took that first step…and secured my spot among the small group of 10 who were selected. Hard work, grit, and perseverance were once again my new buzzwords, and two years later, I was able to hang that degree on my wall, fully prepared to begin my journey as an educational leader.

As for my family, my daughter had her own hurdles starting a new school in a new community. Not only did I have these new job responsibilities and the role of mom and student once again, but we also decided it would be a good time to build a house in a completely different area of the city. I guess we truly embraced the saying "Go big or go home." My daughter, of course, began to find her new friends and continued her path of helping others, while fostering her love of performing. Before long, she once again was thriving daily through middle school.

I remember the morning that I woke up and made the decision that would change my life. Although the new position began to bring me joy and fulfillment, I still wasn't 100% sure I was capable, or even wanted to step into the role of principal. This new position provided me with many opportunities to learn from and collaborate with others in the same role, in addition to some amazing school and district administrators. I not only wondered if I could ever develop the skillset I saw in these people, but if I could actually become a leader like those around me. Could I be a valued and trusted leader that could help a school be its best? Not only did I doubt my skillset, I wasn't sure I could handle the stress of the job. I heard the stories that were discussed—dealing with various student behaviors and parent complaints seemed daunting. Added to that, supervising teachers seemed like a task I was not ready for. Each day I continued to tell myself that although I was on a path of fast growth, I could always stay in this position, feeling completely content. No one could make me become a principal. Until that one morning…

I woke up and started my day as usual. The three of us had our regular morning routine, which consisted of having a quick breakfast together. It was at breakfast that I made the announcement: "I decided I am going to become a principal."

My daughter looked at me and her smile said it all; she could not have been prouder.

My husband simply said, "If that is what you want, we are behind you 100%."

We talked about how much life would change with me taking on this new role. We talked about how great that kind of impact would be. We talked about all I still had to learn in order to make this happen and to do it well. But I was ready! Principal Cheri Dixon…a title I never imagined I would have, but I could now believe it was possible and I was going to do everything I could to make it happen.

I secured my first principal position at a fairly young age. I was now responsible for leading this school to greatness. And that responsibility was massive. I truly had little idea of all that it would take to successfully lead the schools that I was honored to work with, but I learned quickly that a strong leader takes care of their people. They build trusting relationships with those they work with and empower them to do the work, even when it is hard.

Becoming a strong leader also taught me how to be a better mom. Not only did I use my skills to organize and run a school, but I also used them to keep all of life's activities on track. I learned to listen when my daughter had things to discuss. I learned how to help her problem-solve situations, rather than doing it for her. And, being that strong leader, we both learned how to never give up when times are hard. There is always a solution, as long as you never give up.

Running a school, leading any organization, takes time and energy. Being a mom does as well. And then let's throw in the title of wife, and well, I quickly learned that you either run your day or your day runs you. Planning, scheduling, organizing, and great communication were truly needed each and every day of our lives. Many would ask me how I did it. Run the school; have a child in several extracurricular activities; find time to socialize; even fit in training for half marathons. My answer…planning, scheduling, organizing, and great communication.

If I wanted to do all the things, and do them well, I had to take charge and ensure that I was running my day, every day. I have met many women who are completely overwhelmed and stressed due to life's demands. And for many, these women have had to give up their dreams because they just couldn't fit it all in. I get it. Balance is hard, if there really ever is balance. However, when you feel a little more in control of your life, you can feel a little less stressed…and maybe you, too, can find a way to make those dreams a reality!

Every Sunday, we sat as a family and created our calendar. Who had what, when, and where? Who needed transportation to and from? Who could help, if needed? What is the backup plan (always have a backup plan)? We kept this posted so we could all remember, and it was always erasable because the constant thing about life is that there will always be changes. Although my daughter is now 33 years old, and I live alone with my dog, I still use this same system in my life. I am no longer driving children places or keeping up with my husband's schedule, but running a business, writing a book, hosting a podcast and talk show, and creating and producing an upcoming docuseries…either I run my day, or my day runs me.

My time as a principal was one of the most rewarding and challenging times of my life. I can truly say that I accomplished what I set out to do years ago when I woke up one day and decided that it was my path. I was able to develop the skills needed and became the valued and trusted leader who helped schools become their best. I impacted all the little minds and teachers that I worked with over the years, and ultimately left each community in a better place than the first day I entered through the doors.

I said yes…and it made all the difference.

Real-Life Application

1. We all can find ourselves in a place of massive responsibility. As women, we not only lead our families and care for our children but serve as strong female role models to all who are around us daily. I challenge you to ask yourself, how do you show up so that others can say, "If she can do it, so can I?" You don't have to be a formal leader to be someone's role model. As strong women, we already are those role models for others…for our daughters, friends, colleagues, acquaintances. What do you want them to say about you when you leave the room? Do you want them to be inspired to do more, live more, believe more? Do you want them to feel empowered to build a life they love? Take some time to think about this as you continue your journey of improvement.

2. You can run your day, or your day can run you. This is one of my favorite sayings. How do you take charge and run your day? Planning, scheduling, and organizing are great ways to control all the things that come our way each day. I also find that when you are prepared and have a solid plan, when the unexpected comes along—and it always does—you are more prepared to handle it with grace and ease! Let's put this concept into play. I want you to look at your calendar (do you keep one?) for one week. Look at your schedule. Do you have things planned and prioritized? Focus on ensuring that you have a plan for each day, prioritizing the things that matter most. Keep this plan in a place where your family, your tribe, whoever needs to be part of your plan, can see it. Once you have your schedule set, can you do this for your family? Let's see how much less stress and overwhelm you have when you run your day!

CHAPTER 7

Reclaiming My Story: Saying Yes to a New Beginning

I t was an unusually warm day on June 15, 1991, as we headed to my little neighborhood church, ready to make one of the biggest commitments of my life. The day prior, I spent hours with my daughter at the doctor's office, dealing with the residual effects of a previous illness of RSV. At six months of age, she spent two weeks in an oxygen tent in the hospital due to her symptoms, and now we had to work through her lingering asthma-type issues that would periodically arise. The medication issued during this visit was new and didn't sit well with her, so we were back at the emergency room all morning. Not the best start to a wedding day, but we made it to the church and prepared for our beautiful, yet short, ceremony. Before I knew it, we were both saying yes to a lifelong commitment to each other and heading to the party of the year to celebrate our new bond.

I didn't plan to marry Prince Charming. Yes, we dreamed of a life together, a big life together. Yes, he was the one I wanted to have by my side through thick and thin. And yes, he was my best friend, the one I could share my dreams and my fears with. However, we all know the statistics. Teen marriages (yes, I was 20 at the time, but by only a couple of weeks) have a high failure rate, and getting married only because you have a child may sound convenient and appropriate at the time but can truly be a recipe for disaster in the end. I kept thinking that things were perfectly fine between us. We both adored our daughter and wanted her to have that big life, the one in which she could accomplish all of her goals and dreams. I didn't feel we needed that piece of paper to tell us we were a family. But Prince Charming and his family thought differently, so on the cold October day that he proposed, I said yes.

As you can see, we were living our big life. Just as with any marriage, there were great days and days that were a challenge. I worked hard to ensure that we had all we needed, as well as most of our wants, and honestly, created a persona that made the outside world believe that we were the perfect couple. Most of it was real. We loved the same foods, enjoyed similar music, couldn't wait to attend our next social event, and even found similar interests in running and other physical activities. And as I mentioned, we had good times, even what I would sometimes refer to as amazing times in our marriage…until we didn't.

The great times started to become less and less of an occurrence, especially after our daughter went off to college. I kept thinking that this time of our lives would be the time to focus on us, as having married so young, we didn't really have that opportunity from the start. Maybe we would get that Corvette I'd dreamed about so many years ago and spend our weekends exploring the Texas hill country and the plethora of wineries along the way. My husband had a different plan. He thought it would be the perfect time to explore our individual interests. He spent his weekends fishing on Saturdays and drinking with friends on Sundays. I was becoming more of a tag-along if I wanted to spend time with him, and that was not a title I wanted to have. In response, I did what anyone would do: worked a little more, shopped a little more, and spent time with my friends a little more. We were on a path of growing apart, rather than growing together as empty nesters.

I was a bit optimistic, however, at the beginning of June 2010. We were preparing to celebrate our 19th anniversary and my husband took me to dinner to discuss plans for the celebration. He had bought us each a copy of *The 5 Love Languages* and wanted us to read and study it together, which made me believe he wanted us to get back to being a team together. Then he said he had booked us a trip to San Antonio the weekend of our anniversary so we could celebrate together. What I didn't know at the time was that while I thought we were planning a romantic weekend away, he was actually planning a weekend with his friends to drink and party at an Iron Maiden concert, and I got the title of tag-along.

The whole weekend seemed weird to me, even more than usual. I found him stepping away from the group a lot to take phone calls. When I asked him about them, he would just tell me they were work calls, and although I found that strange on the weekend, I wanted to believe him, so I did. When I would initiate a conversation with him, he would respond with brief statements to appease me and revert his attention back to his friends. Even on our actual anniversary night, when I wanted to head back to our hotel and spend time alone together, he wanted to leave me in the room alone to go back and drink on the Riverwalk. Things were just not the same and I knew it, but instead of talking about it, I just let it go in an effort to avoid another one of our numerous disagreements and continued with life.

It just so happened that during the same summer, my grandpa was having some health concerns and I wanted to go home and spend time with him. Being a school leader, although I had hiring and planning to do before the new year began, I found a few days to get away and head back to Iowa. My husband claimed that he just couldn't step away from work at that time, so my daughter and I made the trip together. Once home, I found that many of my high school friends were also visiting, so we not only got to see my grandpa but also had a chance to catch up with my life-long friends. This was something that didn't sit well with my husband, however, and once again, disagreements followed.

It was part way through my vacation that everything in my life changed. My husband stopped responding to my messages and taking my calls. When he would communicate, it was only with our daughter. When I used her phone to contact him, he quickly dismissed me and ended the call. Of course, at that point, he stopped taking calls from her as well. I knew in my gut things were going to get bad...you know when you just have that feeling...and I was right. I needed to get back home quickly and figure out what was happening.

We returned home the next day, and he just wasn't the same. He claimed he was tired from spending time with friends while I was away, and basically worked and came home, going directly to bed for days. It was three days later, as I finished unpacking, doing laundry, and getting on track to head back to school to start the new year when I found the stocking. Completing the last load of laundry, I got to the bottom of the basket and pulled out a long, black, single stocking. My husband was sitting on the other side of the room, so I asked him about the stocking. He quickly replied that he was sure it was mine and why would I think he knew anything about it? My mind began to race frantically. Number one, that stocking was much larger than any size I would wear, and number two, I don't like socks and don't wear them unless it's a must, and I knew it did not belong to me! I responded to him with that information, to which he only could say that I must have picked it up while staying with family. This was also a no...but sadly, my fear overtook me, and I couldn't even continue that conversation. Within days, he admitted that he had been involved with other women and he wanted a divorce. He didn't want to discuss it, he didn't want any of our assets, and he didn't want a therapy session. He only wanted a fast divorce and time to talk to our daughter.

The next hours were hell. The next days were the worst I had ever experienced. The next months were devastating. Lies upon lies flooded every moment of my day. Lies about our marriage. Lies about our separation. Lies about our life. Lies about me. I was hearing things that I thought people only wrote about in books and movies. I experienced public humiliation as my own school community members heard things about me that I could not ever imagine doing (my husband actually hired many of my students' parents at his company over the years, so of course, word travels fast, especially if the word is juicy and involves your child's school principal). And I had to face these people every day while holding it together and successfully running my school. I lost friends. Not because they chose him over me, but when someone close to you gets divorced, you begin to think one of two things: How can we choose a side or still have a normal life with both of them? Is my own marriage headed down this same path and is this a catalyst for our failed future? My life had been turned upside down and I had not wanted any of this.

My anger and fear eventually turned into sadness. I had lost my best friend. I had lost my partner in life. I was alone for the first time in my whole life, and I had no idea what to do. I felt embarrassed by the fact that no matter how hard I tried, I became one of those statistics I'd tried to avoid becoming many years ago. A teenage pregnancy and a marriage due to the fact that a child was born, doomed once again. I began to retreat to my home, avoiding contact with others. I went to work each day, but for quite some time, I was just going through the motions. I started avoiding my feelings by drinking. I began taking sleep aids so I could sleep heavily enough to not dream and replay my sorrows each night. I was a complete mess. This was a place so foreign to me that I didn't even recognize myself, and to be honest, I had no idea how to get back to any kind of normal life.

I wasn't the only one suffering. My daughter was having just as much difficulty with her own feelings. And I know now that I truly was not in a place to help her. I was, however, still a great role model…she saw me and how I was dealing with it all and she started doing the same. It was an extremely dark time in both of our lives, with no end in sight.

On the night I first met my daughter, I vowed that I would be a strong role model, one that would ensure she learned how to build a big, beautiful, and successful life. The day I said yes and stepped into the role of principal, I committed to making the world a better place by ensuring my schools and communities were places that grew successful children into amazing adults. All the times over the years that I said yes and believed that I was capable of building my own big life had been hard work, accompanied by blood, sweat, and tears. And the moment that I realized that I was just stuck in my sorrow, stuck in my circumstances, it hit me. I had come too far to only come this far. I had a choice. I could just stay in this place, living with fear, sorrow, anger, sadness, and embarrassment, and let life determine my future. Or I could do what I needed to do to become whole again, to get comfortable with this uncomfortable time in my life and begin building a brand-new life. One where I put myself first. One where I continued to show my daughter what a strong, confident woman is. One that doesn't let the decisions my husband made shape my own self-worth. One that puts me back on a path that makes my goals and dreams a reality. I knew my future needed to look different and I realized I had to make the choice to take the first step to make it happen.

I said yes…and it made all the difference!

CHAPTER 8

Reclaiming My Power While Reinventing My Identity

I am sure not one of you would be surprised to read that it was reported at the end of 2023 that there were just under 700,000 divorces in the United States. People get divorced. And yes, I am now a confident single woman, post-divorce. But as you also just learned, getting to this level of confidence was not easy, and I know that there are so many women out there struggling just like I was. Anyone can go on various social media platforms and read stories from many of these women, stuck in their own circumstances and not able to move forward. I know that when I was in that place, I almost enjoyed the stuck. Ok, yes, that sounds silly, but it is true. I continually wallowed in my sadness; it gave me an excuse not to move forward. When I shared my tragic story with others (and let me tell you I shared it with anyone who would listen…twice), I got attention. It was not the attention I needed, but it fulfilled my need for attention. And having to face the reality that I had to get uncomfortable when I didn't want to reinforced staying in my pity and just accepting it.

Luckily, I learned many lessons when I had to make hard decisions in life. I learned how to do things even when fear presented itself. I learned to listen to my inner voice, screaming out the endless possibilities when trying something new. And I learned the importance of stepping up as a strong female leader, serving as a positive influence for so many other girls and women in the world. I found myself once again in learning mode.

The first thing that I learned was that there are people out in the world who love it when they can get caught up in someone else's struggle. We all know this is true…and I admit, I can be one of those people at times. How many of us get hooked on the drama of reality TV? When someone else is struggling, it makes us all feel better about our own lives. This is not to say that we don't have sympathy for their struggles, but sometimes their struggles are way bigger than our own and we feel better about our own lives.

I definitely experienced this. People wanted to listen to my drama, and unfortunately, not everyone was listening with the intent of helping me take steps to move forward. And worse yet, some were very motivated to share my sorrows with others. I learned that when you are facing tough times in life, it is imperative that you have a trusted group of people (I can't tell you how many, but I suggest a small number) with whom you can share your story. Find people who truly have your best interest at heart and will support you without spreading your story around town. Find those who will push you and question you when they see that you are stuck in your misery so that you can move forward faster. Remind yourself that this important circle of people only wants the best for you. Once I realized this and found my tribe, I could feel my strength coming back, ready to live again.

I also learned that I was stronger than I'd ever believed. Sure, I am a smart, capable woman who can do a lot of things well, but I was in unknown territory. I had never lived alone in my entire life, which made me think that I was going to be doomed to be lonely for the rest of my life. Pain, suffering, and sadness consumed me, and I started to believe that I was not strong enough to overcome these feelings. It was almost like I was so exhausted that I just didn't have it in me to even consider making a change. I knew I was not taking care of myself physically. I knew my sleep patterns were completely out of control. And it is true what they say about the effect of stress and overwhelm on your body…it will drain you. I remember the moment I knew I was about to embark on this transformation. I was lying on the couch, flipping through the channels mindlessly, and started thinking about the fact that when someone has a solid workout plan, they actually gain more energy. Many people think that doing this strenuous exercise when you are already tired makes you more tired, but the opposite is true—you gain energy. It's like I often say: Physical exercise is like free therapy. And it was time for me to apply that to my own life once again.

I started working out again. I started putting my mind on more productive activities during my free time. I started socializing again (new friends, but ones who are now permanently in my circle). And I stayed off the couch! I quickly saw a change. Maybe it was my mindset. Maybe it was the realization that, although different, I could have a fulfilling life again. Or maybe I was just keeping myself busy and not allowing time to get caught up in my story. Whatever it was, I began to find my strength again. I started to feel joy again. I learned what I wanted my life to look like, on my terms. It felt amazing…and I found myself smiling again.

When you experience a major setback in life, it will rock you to your core. It can make you question everything about yourself and all the hard work you have done to get to where you are. It can make you sad, angry, fearful, and overwhelmed. But digging deep and remembering the great things about yourself can keep you motivated to stay out of the "stuck" and get on a path of rebuilding.

I was allowing the actions of my husband to determine my future. It took realizing that no matter how many times I told that story, no matter how awful I felt because of him, and how angry I was with his actions, I could not control his choices. I could only control my response…and I wasn't doing that. I was stuck and doing all I could to "change" what he did—until I had a talk with myself and reminded myself that I get to choose how I show up, I get to choose how I respond. And I wanted to choose a life of fulfillment, big things, and a whole lot of class. I stopped telling the story. I stopped asking myself what I could have possibly done to deserve what had happened. I started dressing differently. I changed my hair to a style I wanted. I changed my makeup to allow me to feel better about my appearance. I guess you can say I found my brand. The one that told people exactly what I started to feel on the inside…that when I walk into the room, I am confident, courageous, and clear, and I was ready to live my life on my terms.

Divorce was one of the toughest things I have gone through in my life. Not only did I lose my best friend and many of my other friendships, but I lost myself. What I didn't understand at the time was that I had to lose it all to know what I wanted my life to be for me. The most important lesson I learned on this journey was that I am worthy of having a life that I love; that this experience didn't define who I am (and it shouldn't for you either), but it did provide me an opportunity to reinvent myself and find my true identity!

I said yes…and it made all the difference!

Reflection

1. When tough times arise, it is easy to get consumed in the feelings we all can experience. We continually ask ourselves why this is happening. We stay focused on wondering what we could have done differently so that we could have avoided this situation. And, many times, we stay stuck, replaying the situations over and over in our minds and sharing them with anyone who will listen.

   If you find yourself in a situation like this, it may be time to take the first step to move out of your circumstance and let go so you can continue living a great life. We cannot control what happened, only how we respond. Let's begin to respond without allowing this experience to determine our future. What is the first step you need to take to begin moving on? This step may be uncomfortable, and that's ok. The uncomfortable feeling will begin to become comfortable the more you do it. Hold yourself accountable for it. Then you can determine step 2, 3, and, one day soon, you will be back on track, building a life you love!

2. Self-confidence and self-worth are two different concepts. When we have confidence, we can allow ourselves to show up in a way that communicates to the world that we have the knowledge and skills to do the work and we feel comfortable doing it. Self-worth is our belief that we deserve to have what we want in life. We all want both, but I find that the feeling of worthiness can be harder to attain. Do you feel you are worthy of having a life you love, one that allows you to accomplish your goals and dreams? If you don't, let's reflect

on this. Is it an experience you had that makes you doubt yourself? Is it a person whose actions are affecting your own feelings? Once you understand why you feel unworthy, you can then determine how to change this. Take time to reflect on this, so you can build your dream life in the future.

CHAPTER 9

Turning the Page at 50: Finding My Purpose and Passion in Midlife

Twenty-eight, sixteen, thirteen, fifty, two, and nine…numbers that play a significant role in my life. *She Said Yes and It Made All the Difference* was released on May 28, 2024, my 53rd birthday! I love my birthday! Actually, I love the entire month of May, and not just because amazing people were born in this month! May signifies the end of spring and the start of summer. May brings sunny, warm weather. May is the wrap-up of the school year, celebrating all the hard work everyone in the school community has accomplished. May brings high school graduations, releasing motivated young adults who are anxious to make their mark on the world. And I celebrate another trip around the sun!

I graduated high school on May 28. I started my business on May 28. And now, my first solo book was released on May 28. It's a great day! But that's not the only significance of twenty-eight. I served several communities as an educator for 28 years. I was a teacher, an instructional specialist, a district-level coordinator, an assistant principal, and a principal. Looking back on my career, I am sometimes amazed at the impact I have had. I am always honored to know that I shaped our future and those of each of the communities where I serve. And I loved every position I held along the way. I consider myself one of the lucky ones... I got to do a job I loved for all those years!

For 16 years, I have had the title of principal. Wow...it sounds like a long time as I write this, but the time flew by. Over those years, I led three different schools, in three different districts, in two different states. Each had its own personality, processes, and procedures, making them unique. However, they all had one thing in common: When I became the principal at each school, it was in a state of failure. The academic achievement of students was low. The discipline referrals were high. And teachers were coming and going frequently, resulting in a concerning turnover rate. I was brought into each one, charged with fixing the problems quickly and getting the school back on a path of success. I accomplished my mission at each one, but only because I learned how to lead people, motivate children, coach teachers, and build relationships within the school community. Each school not only needed a turnaround, but each one was located in a low socioeconomic area with a diverse population, presenting other needs as well. I was there to serve. I vowed to build schools that were successful. I was on a mission to ensure I helped make the school community the best it could be. And I loved every minute of it!

I have now been divorced for 13 years. Sometimes it seems like I went through that challenging time just yesterday, and sometimes it feels like it was an eternity ago. Over the last 13 years, I have learned what makes me happy. I have found my way forward as a single woman. I have enjoyed new friendships and some romantic partnerships as well. I have built a mother-daughter bond with my wonderful, beautiful, amazing, successful 30-something-year-old daughter, the one I believed could be possible the day I met her. And I am definitely living my dream life. As I look back, I know that all the experiences in my life have shaped me into the person I am. The knowledge and wisdom gained in my 50s have completely prepared me for the ups and downs of my current path and, most importantly, I have learned the importance of building a life that aligns with my core values, brings me joy and fulfillment, and gives me the courage to live as my authentic self. I couldn't have understood this at 30-something, or even at 40-something. I am truly aging gracefully and living my big life!

Turning 50 did present a hurdle for me. I started to get a bit antsy. I began wondering the what-ifs. What if I had chosen a different career path? What if I moved and started over somewhere new? What if…? I could feel it. I needed a change. My midlife crisis was popping up and I needed to address it. My life was pretty amazing. I had a very successful career. I had all I wanted and more…the car, the dream house, the shoes…and for a moment I couldn't figure it out, but I felt stuck.

All that I had didn't come easy. I worked hard to get where I was. I dedicated my time to my career. I continuously took care of others' needs before my own. I was living, but I realized I was not living for me. I hadn't had time for a vacation….not a trip to Iowa to visit family, not a quick weekend getaway before racing back to work…but a real vacation in years. Yes, I have things that made my life look very glamorous on the outside, but I was feeling the spark beginning to go out on the inside. I was longing for more.

Shortly after I began to question my life path, a close friend of mine lost her husband very unexpectedly. I spent some time with her after it happened and realized that life is too short. We cannot even begin to know when our last day on earth will be. And with all the questions I had about my own path, I began to wonder if, were my own life to end suddenly, would I have regret? Would I have wished that I had listened, once again, to the inner voice that was pushing me to make a change in my life? If I did consider change, what could I possibly do next? Sure, I had a great education coupled with amazing experiences, but would people still see me as an educator, stifling my progress in a new field? I was a big fish in the small pond of education. At the age of 50, was I ready to be a guppy again in a sea of something new? Something in me also kept thinking, do I want to make a change just to go work for someone else once again? Or was it time to build my own empire…a legacy for me and my family? A chance to build my reputation as a valued and trusted business owner, courageous enough to make this pivot, even when scared.

Two years ago, I announced my own business to the world! Of course, I did it in a very "Carrie Bradshaw, *Sex and the City*" fashion. My closest friends helped me celebrate the start of something completely new! I took courses to become certified as a life coach and I was on a mission to impact 5,000 women over the next 10 years by supporting them as they developed the courage to build and live their dream lives. I became an author, releasing my first chapter in the book *Unleash Her* in October of 2022. I said yes to totally stepping out of my comfort zone and creating and hosting my own online talk show (and it won an award for season one)! Balancing this new life while still running my school was hard. I started to not just wonder "What if," but began telling myself, "When I do it," and planned to do this new adventure full-time. So many emotions filled my being once again: excitement for the possibilities, fear of failure, curiosity about what this path could lead to, and a lot of unrest. I felt like I was cheating on public education. I felt that I had come so far in my career, and I would miss the work so much. But I felt it was time for this change. I was not getting younger, days are not promised, and I found the courage to step away and make an even bigger life my reality! And, two years later, I packed my office, hugged the students and families on the last day of school, and shed tears with my fabulous staff.

I said yes…and it made all the difference!

I Said Yes...and It Made All the Difference!

A s I finish this final chapter in my first book and prepare to send it off to the publisher, I am also wrapping up my ninth month of being an entrepreneur. Nine...nine months ago I walked out of my school office and began a new adventure. And, to be honest, there are days when I say to myself (or my business partner, my 12-year-old chocolate lab-pitbull— he doesn't answer back so he is the perfect sounding board), "What the hell were you thinking???"

The first couple of months were quite an adjustment. I had to rethink my schedule, on my terms. I had to rethink my brand, and of course, it's pink, sparkly, and fabulous. I had to rethink everything I did for my business. At a school, you open the doors, and the customers come running in, literally. Not the same when starting a business. Yes, my friends, family, and small network knew about my pivot, but I now had to tell the world. Plus, I had to do it in a way that was authentic and made me look like I knew what I was doing so people would pay me for my services.

I mentioned that I was on the path of being a life coach for women. Well, that changed a few months in. I missed the work I did with struggling schools and quickly realized that running a school is no different than running any organization (our customers were just younger, shorter, and required guidance on the playground). So, I adjusted my brand, my message, and my services to help small businesses build and grow, and, most recently, to empower female leaders to develop their skills to take on big jobs and make amazing things happen within their organizations.

Money didn't flow in on a consistent basis. Some months were good, some were awful. I learned a whole lot about the healthcare marketplace and became the proud owner of a health insurance policy that I now must actually pay for to keep valid. I had to learn a system for tracking expenses, saving receipts, and so many other things related to running a business, none of which I'd had to do as a principal (they gave me a secretary for that). I developed systems for acquiring clients, only to learn that I needed to adjust because they weren't working as I had hoped. By a few months in, I was exhausted, overwhelmed, and doubting if I could really make this happen.

I promised myself that I would not quit and reminded myself that I don't usually fail…and kept telling myself I was that small guppy in this big ocean. I vowed to persevere and not give up or go right back to the world of education. So, I sat down and remembered all the lessons I had learned when I had to make a hard decision, said yes, and it truly did make all the difference.

1. Your childhood will shape who you are as an adult, but it doesn't define you.
2. Making a change or taking a step forward in a new direction can be scary, but we can do big things, even when afraid.

3. Listen to that inner voice, the one cheering you on when you are out making your dreams come true.
4. Our mind is powerful, and it can convince us that we can or can't. We need to learn to control our mind and quiet it when it tells us we can't.
5. As a leader, we have influence on those who come up behind us. We need strong female leaders who give us hope that if they can do it, so can we.
6. Formal leadership is a massive responsibility, but as women, we also serve as a leader to our families and our children. Developing your skills could make you better in all areas of life.
7. Bad things happen to good people, and sometimes we may not understand why. We cannot control what happens, but we can control how we respond, not letting life determine our future.
8. Actions of others do not define us and do not determine our self-worth. Understand that you are worthy of a great life, one on your terms, and make it your reality.

Suddenly, I started to remember why I had started this journey. That led me to focus on the amazing things that were happening.

- My talk show was a success and I started Season 2.
- My clients were making so much growth which left them satisfied with my services.
- I had an opportunity to write for two anthologies before writing this book.
- I also led a group of exceptional educators in our own anthology, *The Heroes in Our Classrooms*, which was released on May 7, 2024.

- I created and released my first docuseries (a long-time dream) about navigating the world of autism, *Somewhere on the Spectrum.*
- I am continuing to have an impact on women all over the world with my services and support.
- And, I have learned a lot! More than I ever imagined I would…in a short amount of time.

So, what has this final journey that I shared with you taught me? Average people can do amazing things in life. You do not need to be born into "the right family" to make your goals and dreams a reality. You do not need to have a list of college degrees to have an impact on the world. You do not need to be perfect at something to start something new. You just need the desire to make your dream a reality, the faith that it is possible, a detailed plan that will give you the steps to success, and a way to hold yourself accountable for executing that plan. Simple, right? Don't overthink it. Some of the most amazing products and services in the world today were developed in just this way.

I sat down, remembered my why, and realized that I had a burning desire to make this dream real. I'm not giving up. I may need a detour every once in a while, but the legacy I will build will be exactly what I envision it to be!

I believe this is 100% possible for me. My faith in myself, my abilities, and my plan is so strong that it will work. And I know that if it doesn't, I have the ability to adjust the plan…not quit on the plan or on myself. As a matter of fact, I have so much faith in this new stage of my life that I actually got the word *faith* tattooed on my arm the day after I left my school office. If that is not commitment, I don't know what is!

Plans are the roadmap to our finish line. Without one, we will just be wandering around, hoping things will happen. I am a planner. My roadmap is set for the next week, month, year…even five years out. Sure, things change, and it may need to be altered, but the map is there. It gives me direction in all that I'm doing, and I would be lost without it.

Living life with intention has always been a goal for me. I intentionally schedule things that need to happen. I intentionally plan my individual personal and professional development each year. I even intentionally plan out time to connect with family and friends. Then I hold myself accountable. Starting my business was no different. I built that beautiful roadmap. I spent hours ensuring that I had a plan for success. I sure don't have time to have wasted that time putting this all together. I need to execute and do each step along the way to get closer and closer to my dream. Checklists are my best friend. Scheduled review and reflection on my actions are a must. It sounds like a lot, but this is truly one piece in it all that has made all those amazing things that I have experienced so far in my business a reality.

It is now time for my final lesson on this journey with you. These are all lifelong lessons that will continue to move me forward in life, but this one especially, as a 50-something-year-old woman experiencing life changes, physically, emotionally, and based on all my dreams: You are never too old to start something new. When I took my first step as an entrepreneur, I started developing a program for middle-aged women who were stuck in life after their children left the nest, they hit the ceiling in their career, or suddenly found themselves single after years of marriage. As I prepared that program and conducted my research, the number one concern women like me reported was that they were feeling stuck because they felt irrelevant. I found this to be such a profound thought, and with all transparency, I felt it, too.

When I was younger, I was a fast up-and-comer in my career. I began college as a physical education major and my physical health and appearance have always been a priority for me. Not only that, but back in the day, I had the home that everyone wanted to hang out at. As I came into my adult persona, I found that not only was I living big in the city…but I was living large, a life others would have loved to have.

Mid-life changes you! Sure, you truly have more knowledge, wisdom, maturity…but your body changes. Relationships change over the years as well. And outfits you could once pull off in your young, cute, ultra-fit body may be frowned upon now. This may not resonate with everyone, but if you are a middle-aged woman reading this, you know what I mean. That feeling of irrelevance is real!

It truly took me two years to build up the courage to step away from my world of education to embark on this new journey. There have been times when I walked into the room and wondered if those present questioned my ability due to my age or the number of years spent in my previous role. And I cannot even tell you how many people question why I would pivot at this age. But I know I do not want to live life with regret. I do not want to just accept a future in which I am unfulfilled because I am too old to change. You *can* teach an old dog new tricks, and I have learned that the only time we fail is when we give up on our hopes and dreams.

I have a ways to go before I can say I will be at the same level professionally in this business as I was in the world of education. It took me years to develop the value and trust others saw in me in that world, and I am ready to put in the work and time it will take me in the world of business as well. The road is not ending anytime soon for me, so look out world, here I come!

And I wrap up with this: If this once shy and intimidated girl from small-town Iowa can leap over the hurdles that I have experienced, gain the knowledge and wisdom from all the lessons, and have the courage to build a life I love, you can too!

I said yes…and it made all the difference!

Reflection

There are many people in the world who give up on their hopes and dreams every day. Yes, it is hard, but this may not be why they give up. It could be that they don't have a plan to make things happen. Or, they don't know how to hold themselves accountable. Maybe they believe they need a certain background or need to be a celebrity before taking that next step. And many believe they are just too old to make the change.

What about you? Are you living your dream life? What is stopping you? I share my stories and the lessons I have learned in this book so that you can have this knowledge and wisdom in hopes that you will build your dream life, too! Allow yourself to dream! Allow yourself to set big goals! Use my experiences to guide you on your path to accomplishing them, living your life with intention, and building your big life!

I would love to hear from you! You can find me on all the social media platforms. Drop me a message and let me know what you are building in your life so I can cheer you on!

Go say yes! It will make all the difference!

Spread Our Message!

She Said Yes…And It Made All the Difference

With Cheri Dixon Consulting, LLC

Cheri Dixon Consulting, LLC was formed in June of 2023, after Cheri left her career of 28 years in public education. Cheri always knew she wanted to impact the lives of others and now works with female leaders to continue to develop their skills so that they can produce unlimited success in their organizations. The leader is truly key to success, and many female leaders just need that little extra support to help them build their skill set so that they can feel confident to step into those high-level positions and become the leader they were meant to be!

Are You Looking to Build Your Leadership Skills?

Cheri Dixon Consulting offers a variety of supports for aspiring and experienced leaders that will ensure that they are able to flourish in their career.

Are you an aspiring or current school leader and want the right cheerleader by your side so you can level up your skills and take your organization from average to amazing? Email me and let's schedule a call to discuss your journey and how we can work together to get you on your path to unimaginable success!

cheri@cheridixonconsulting.com

Visit cheridixonconsulting.com to see how YOU can build a life you love, fulfilling all your goals and dreams personally and professionally!

Have you checked out the *Strong: Inside and Out Podcast?*

Find me on Apple and Spotify Podcasts!

Join me on my journey in the world of media!

Not only can you catch my talk show, *Confident, Courageous and Clear with Cheri*, but you can find my first documentary, *Somewhere on the Spectrum: Navigating the World of Autism*!

Visit <u>Fenix TV</u> for details!

About the Author

Cheri Dixon is the owner of Cheri Dixon Consulting LLC, which she started after leaving a 28-year career in public education. Cheri lives in Houston and now takes her work into the business world, helping businesses scale their organizations to the next level. Cheri believes that the leader is crucial to success and supports leaders to develop their skills to strive for excellence in this global society. Cheri is an international best-selling author, and podcast host, and has an award-winning talk show. Cheri loves spending time with her daughter, her chocolate lab-pitbull, and running her yearly half marathon!

LinkedIn: https://www.linkedin.com/in/cheri-dixon-38938b244/

Facebook: https://www.facebook.com/cheri.dixon.35

Instagram: https://www.instagram.com/cheridixonconsulting/

Website: https://www.cheridixonconsulting.com